Teacher Jeanette
GETTING STARTED
with Alphabet & Numbers

a Primer for Beginners
Teacher's Edition

Ophelia S. Lewis

Village Tales Publishing

MINNEAPOLIS, MN

Copyright © 2023 by Ophelia S. Lewis
All rights reserved. No part of this publication may be reproduced, distributed or transmitted in any form or by any means, without prior written permission.

Village Tales Publishing
www.villagetalespublishing.com
www.oass.villagetalespublishing.com
www.villagetalespublishing.com/childrensbooks

Book Cover and formatting by OASS
ISBN: 9781959580010
Library of Congress Control Number: 2023910923

A Liberia Literary Society
Educational Project

Printed in the USA

This book belongs to:

_____

How to care for your book.

1. Read with clean hands.
2. Turn pages carefully.
3. Keep your book in your bookbag when you're not reading it.
4. Keep your book close to you when reading, so that you don't drop it.
5. Use a bookmark to save your page in a book.
6. Keep your book away from food and drinks.
7. Only draw, write, and color where instructed to.
8. Keep your book away from younger siblings and pets.

Primary Handwriting Guidelines

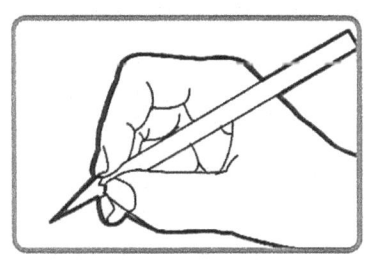

Sit down and place book flat in front of you.

Use your helper hand to hold the paper down while writing.

Correctly hold your pencil; only move the fingers when writing.

Notes on the Contributors

Manseen Logan is a Liberian-American editor and writer. She published the first story in the "Adventures at Camp Pootie-Cho" children's book series. In the series, readers can learn about Liberia's endangered wildlife, the unique rainforest, and valuable life lessons. She enjoys participating in kids' book readings sponsored by Liberia Literary Society.

Patrice Juah is a communications professional, writer and editor. As founder of the Martha Juah Educational Foundation, she champions girls' education and leadership, through the foundation's academic initiative, Sexy Like A Book. An accomplished author, poet, and public speaker, her literary works cover a wide range of themes, to include personal life experiences, women's empowerment and humor. A firm believer in the transformative power of education, Juah contributes to the Liberia Literary Society and Village Tales Publishing, as board member and editor, respectively.

Ophelia S. Lewis is the CEO of the Liberia Literary Society organization, which provides resources to preserve Liberia's literary works, advance girls' education and youth development. Giving children a chance to learn is one of the most urgent priorities in Liberia. As a published author and humanitarian, Lewis takes on the dire, yet fulfilling task of giving children an opportunity to start a solid educational journey. Hopefully, the synergy of Liberia Literary Society and Village Tales Publishing will produce effective results for students. Quality education is key to any society's success; this ignites Lewis' passion for writing children's books.

Teacher Jeanette Kinder Kollege workbooks are packed with exercises that will make learning fun! These workbooks will provide a gentle introduction to structured learning that is both developmentally appropriate and academically foundational. They are proven activities to help prepare Liberian students for success; by teaching strong fundamentals to start their educational journey. Students will LOVE learning.

Introduction

The first thing we teach preschoolers is letters and counting because these skills are foundational to all knowledge they'll acquire through the year. However, the first thing we introduce on the first day of school should be 'mindset'. What does mindset mean? To put it simply, mindset is a way of thinking. Before learning the alphabet, introduce the word mindset to your students. Mindset is the way we think. They don't need to understand the importance of their way of thinking, or worldview right now, but you need to show them how to use their brain (think). It will define how they look at the world, approach things, and behave when faced with difficult or unexpected situations. Our mindset influences how we think, feel, and behave in any given situation. It means that what we believe about ourselves impacts our success or failure. The Teacher's Edition has an entire section on how to teach students about mindset.

Pre-Kindergarten is the foundation of a child's education. The educational "house" a child builds in his/her life will be built on the foundation of pre-kindergarten. It is during the first years of life that children form attitudes about themselves, others, learning, and the environment. Educating a child is most successful when teachers and schools work together in the best interest of the child. Valuing education and the opportunities it provides are important first steps.

Teacher Jeanette Kinder Kollege workbooks are packed with exercises that will make learning fun! These workbooks will provide a gentle introduction to structured learning that is both developmentally appropriate and academically foundational. They are proven activities to help prepare Liberian students for success; by teaching strong fundamentals to start their educational journey. Students will LOVE learning.

Contents

Introduction	viii
The Alphabet	13
Trace the Uppercase Letters	40
Trace the Lowercase Letters	41
I Can Write My ABC's	42
Connect the dots from A — Z	78
More Alphabet Pratice	83
Phonics Sounds Worksheets	100
Kindergarten Sight Word List	116
Numbers	129
Teen Numbers	143
Trace the numbers.	145
Writing Numbers Practice	146
Numbers 1-50	156
Numbers 51-100	157
Fill in the Missing Numbers	158
Learn your number words	160
Write Your Number Word	161
Color by Number	174
Color by Number Word	177
Under the Sea	178
Shapes and Colors	181
Color Words	188

Mixing Some Colors 212
Growth Mindset — what is it? 213
Teaching growth mindset to young students 221
Character Building 222
Being Independent..225
Good Character Vocabulary..226
Good Manners Alphabet 228
52 Bible Verses to Memorize 230
Safety..233
Motivating With Passion 235
How to be a Great Teacher 237
Empowering Students...239
Academic Journal 245
No Child Left Behind 253
Primer Spelling List...256

TEACHERS PLANT SEEDS THAT GROW FOREVER

CLASSROOM RULES

POSITIVE MINDSET

OPEN MIND

Keep Our Classroom Clean.

Listen Carefully and Follow Directions.

LOVE PEACE

Respect Yourselves and Others.

Be positive

TAKE CARE OF YOUR MIND

Have a Good Attitude and Work Hard.

Arrive On Time and Be Prepared For Class.

I can
IMPROVE
if I keep
TRYING

I will not give up!

I know things can get better!

I know I can learn new things!

I Can!

The Alphabet
My Brain is Ready to Grow!

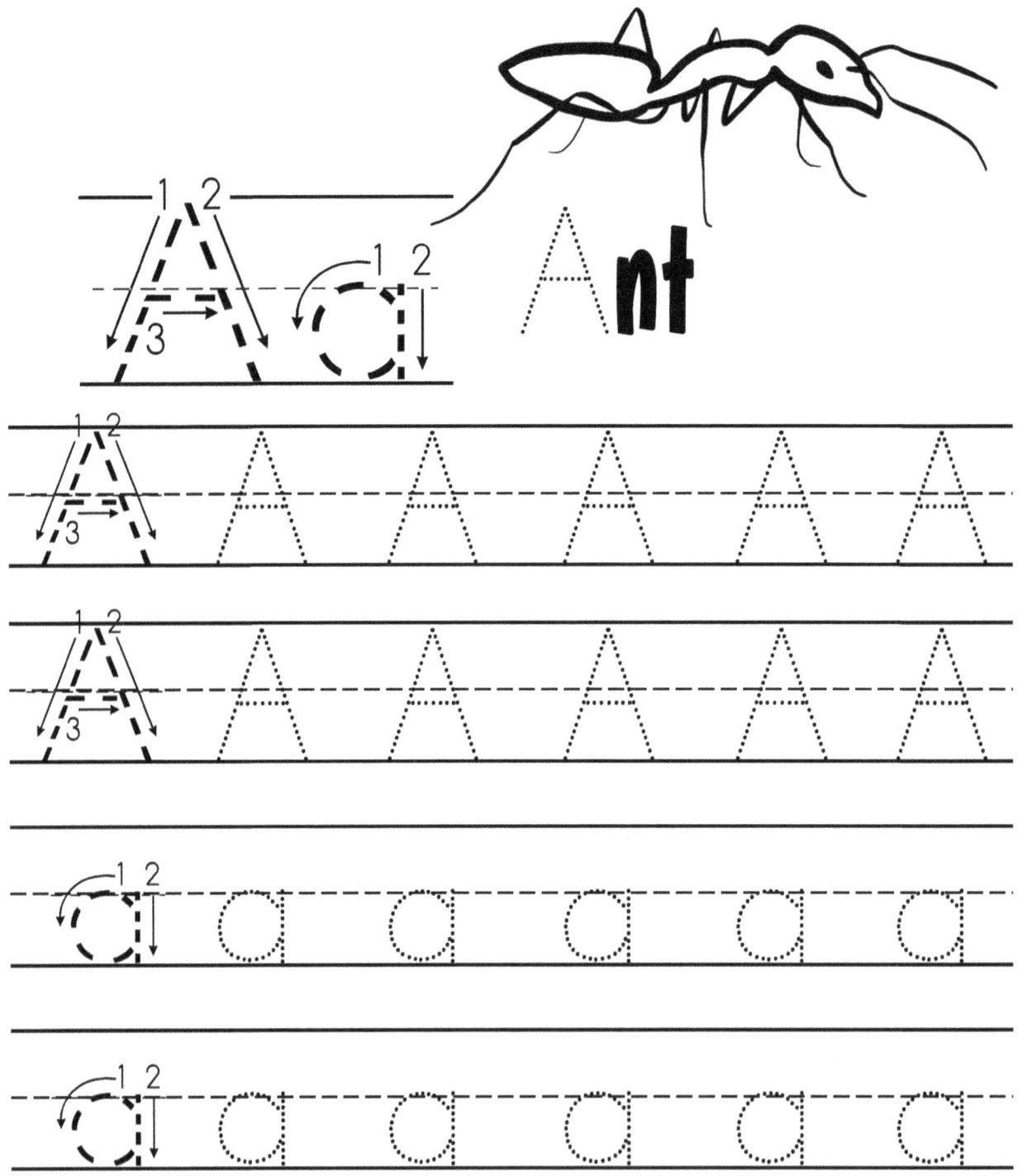

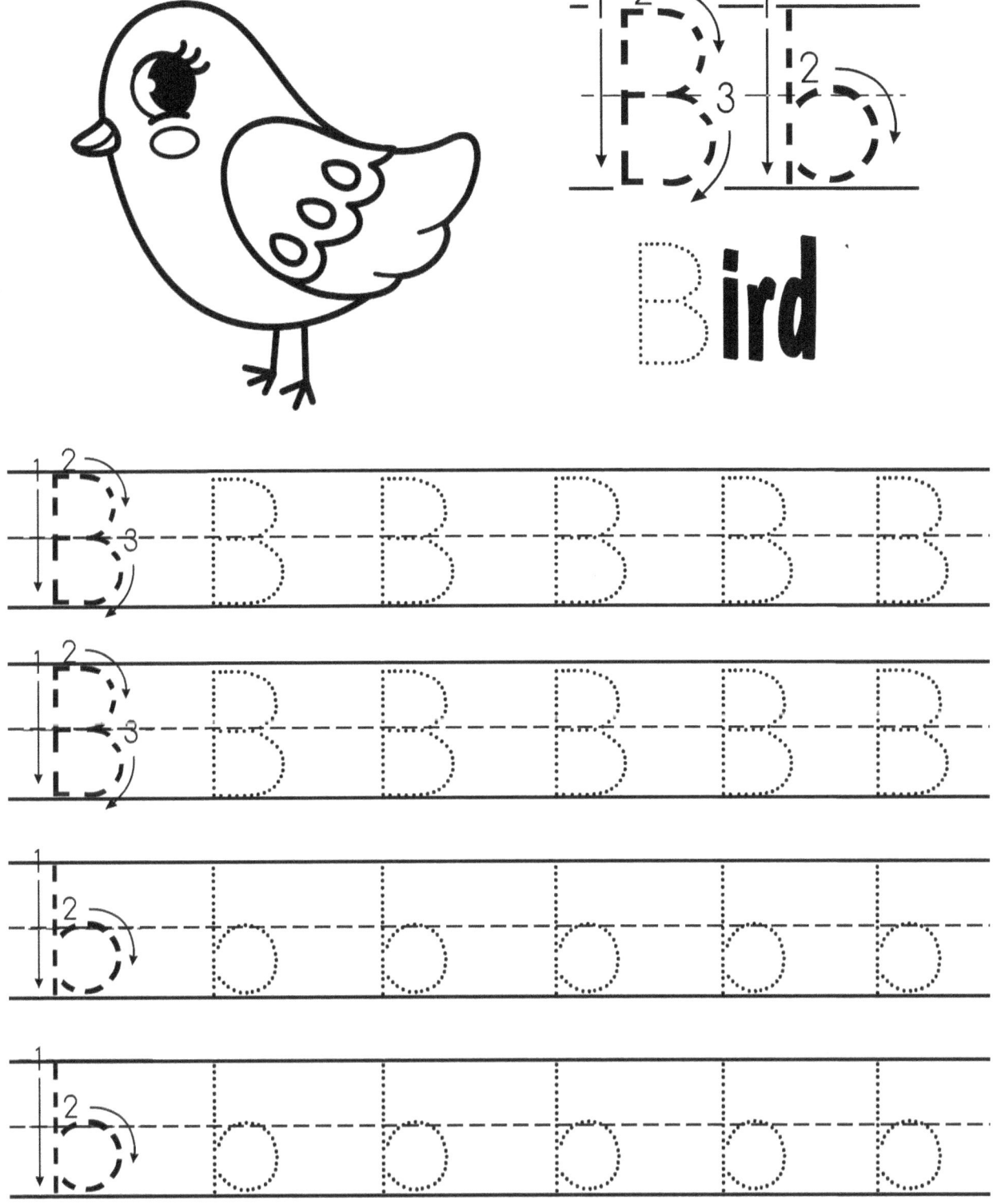

Bird

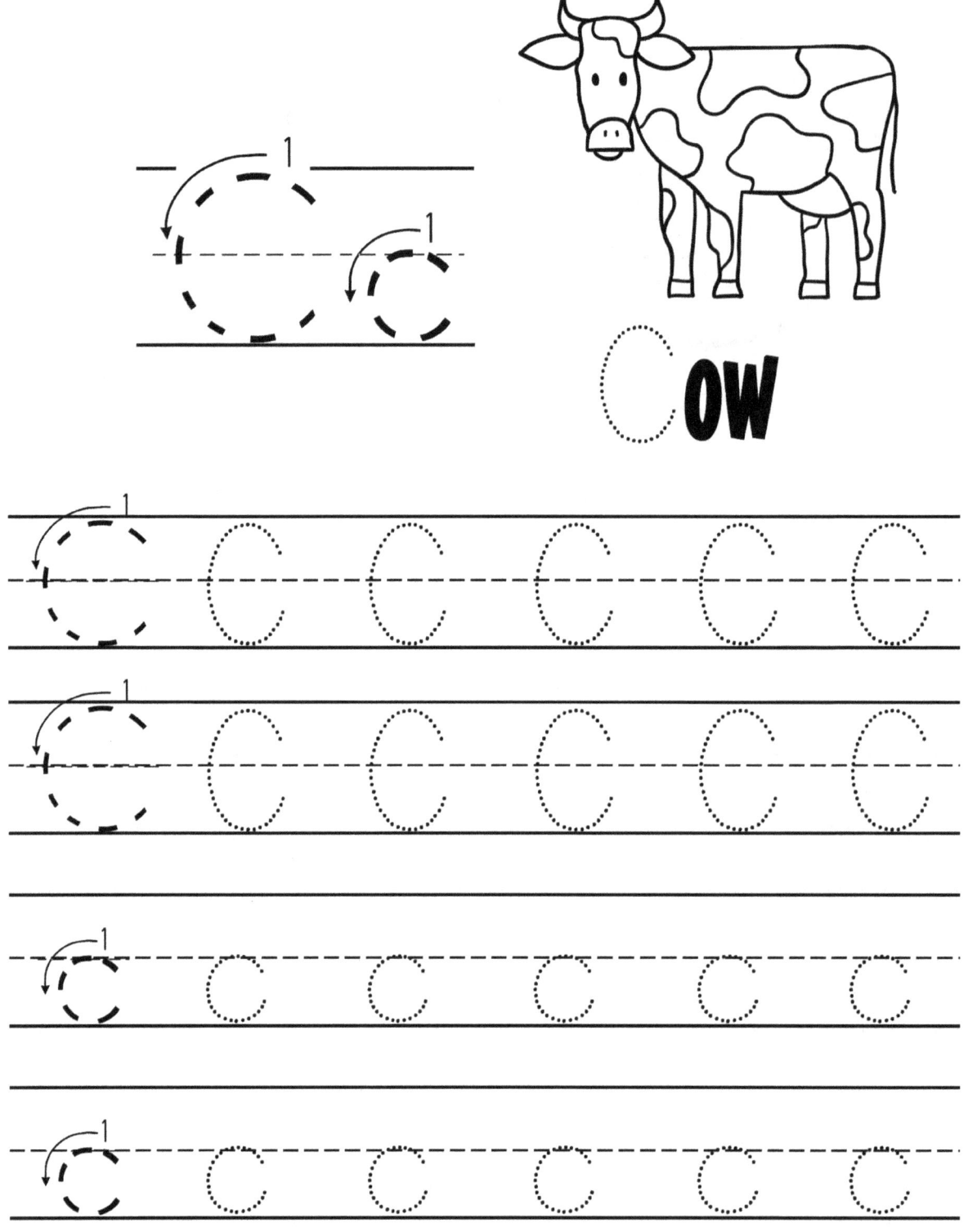

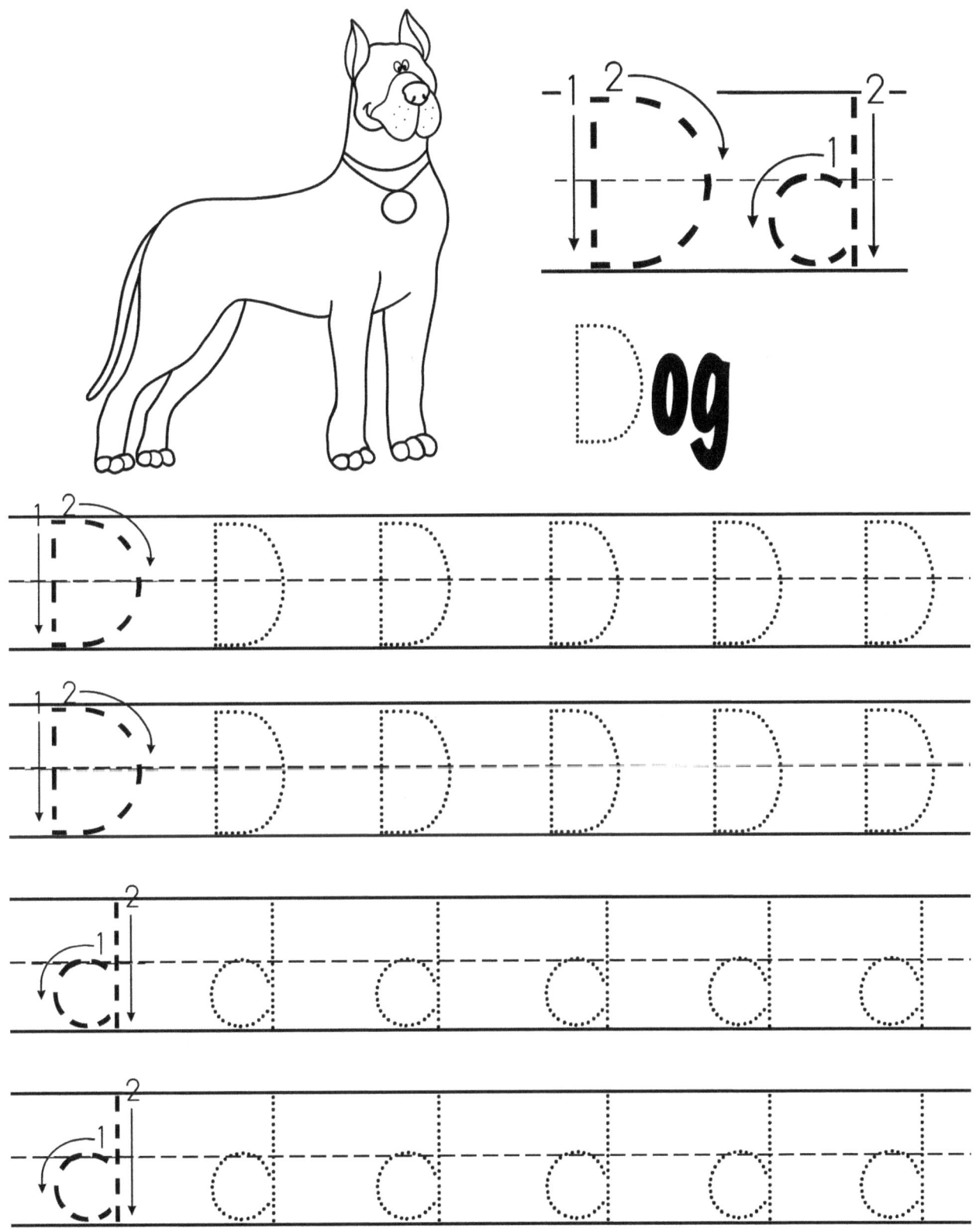

Egg

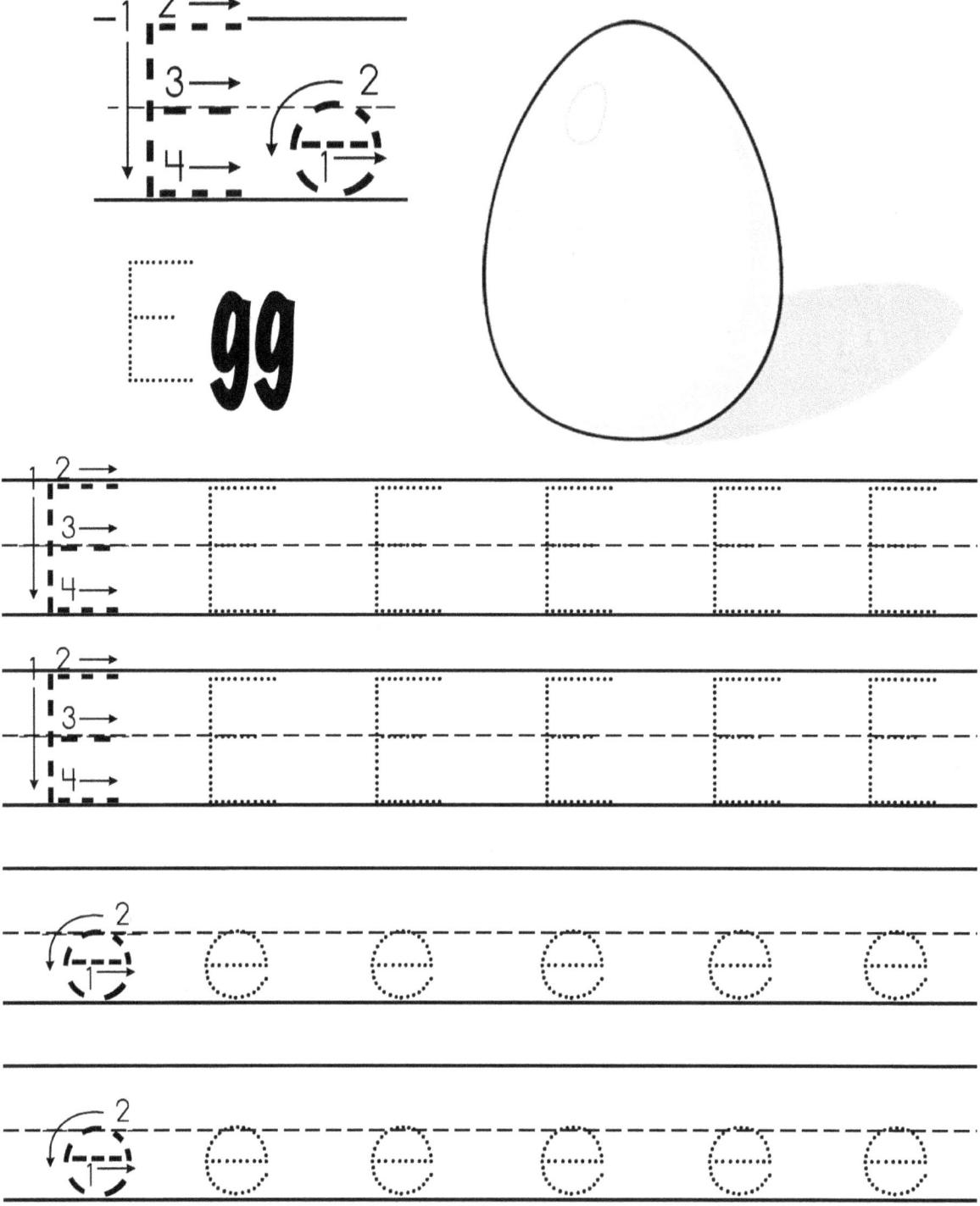

18

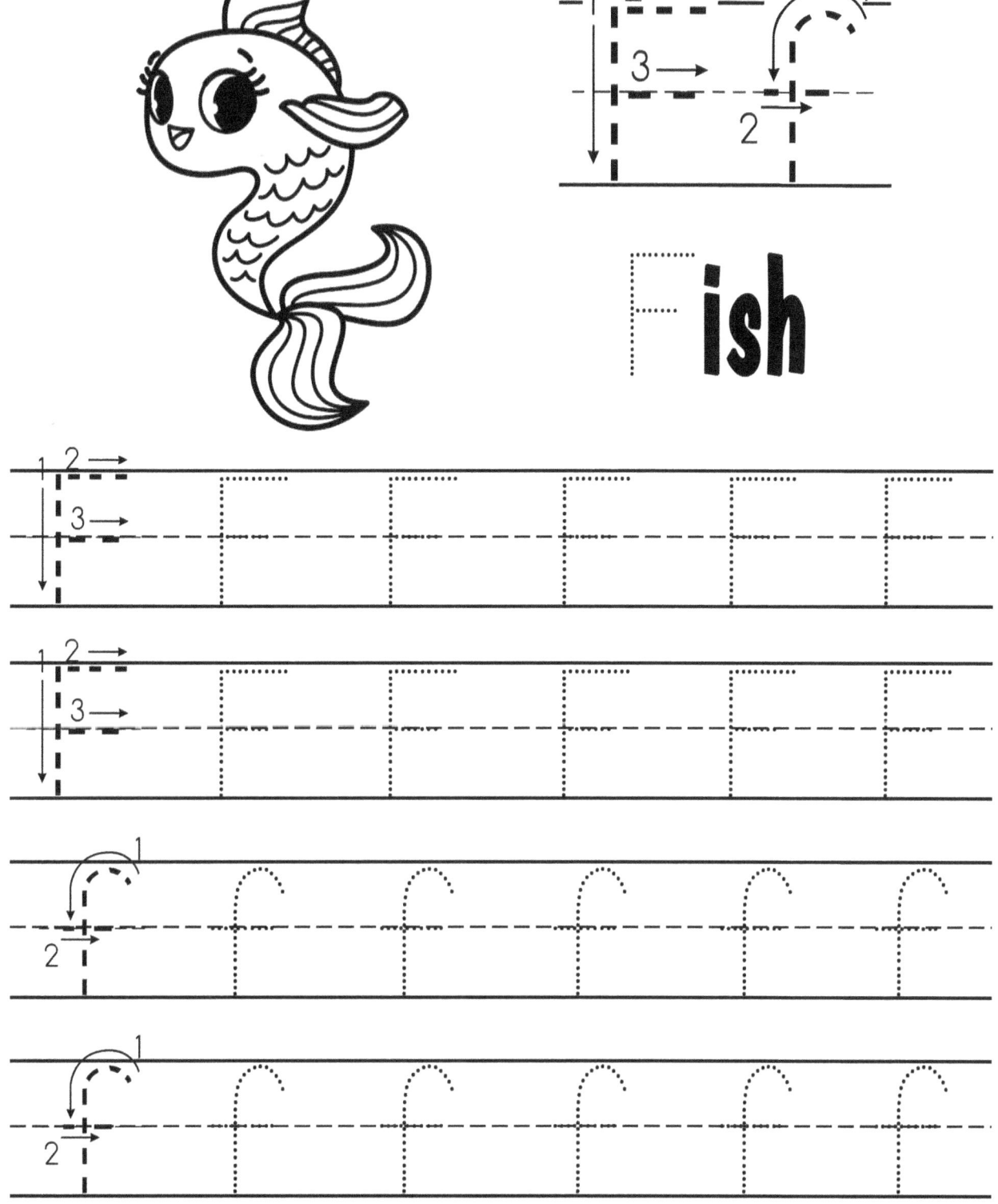

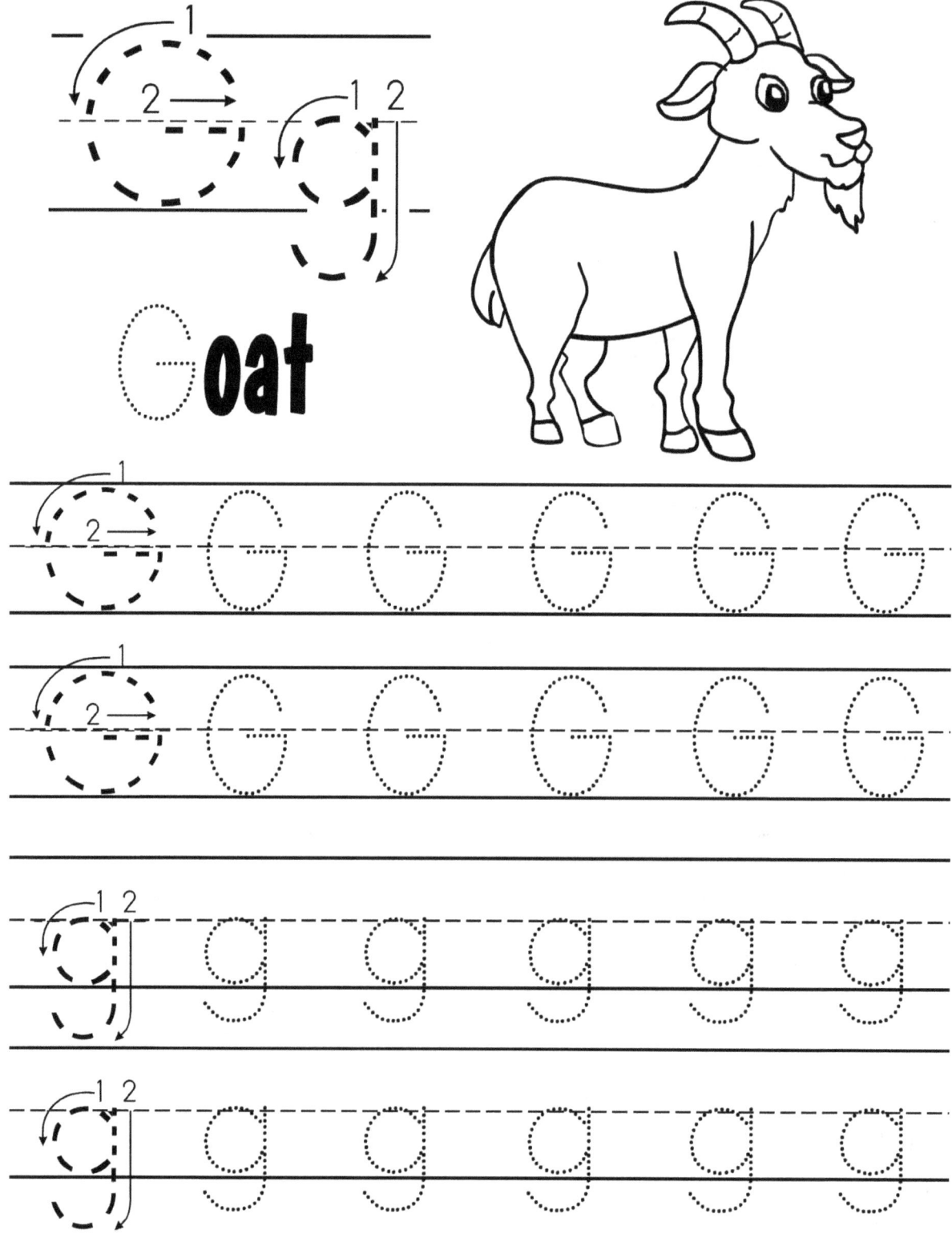

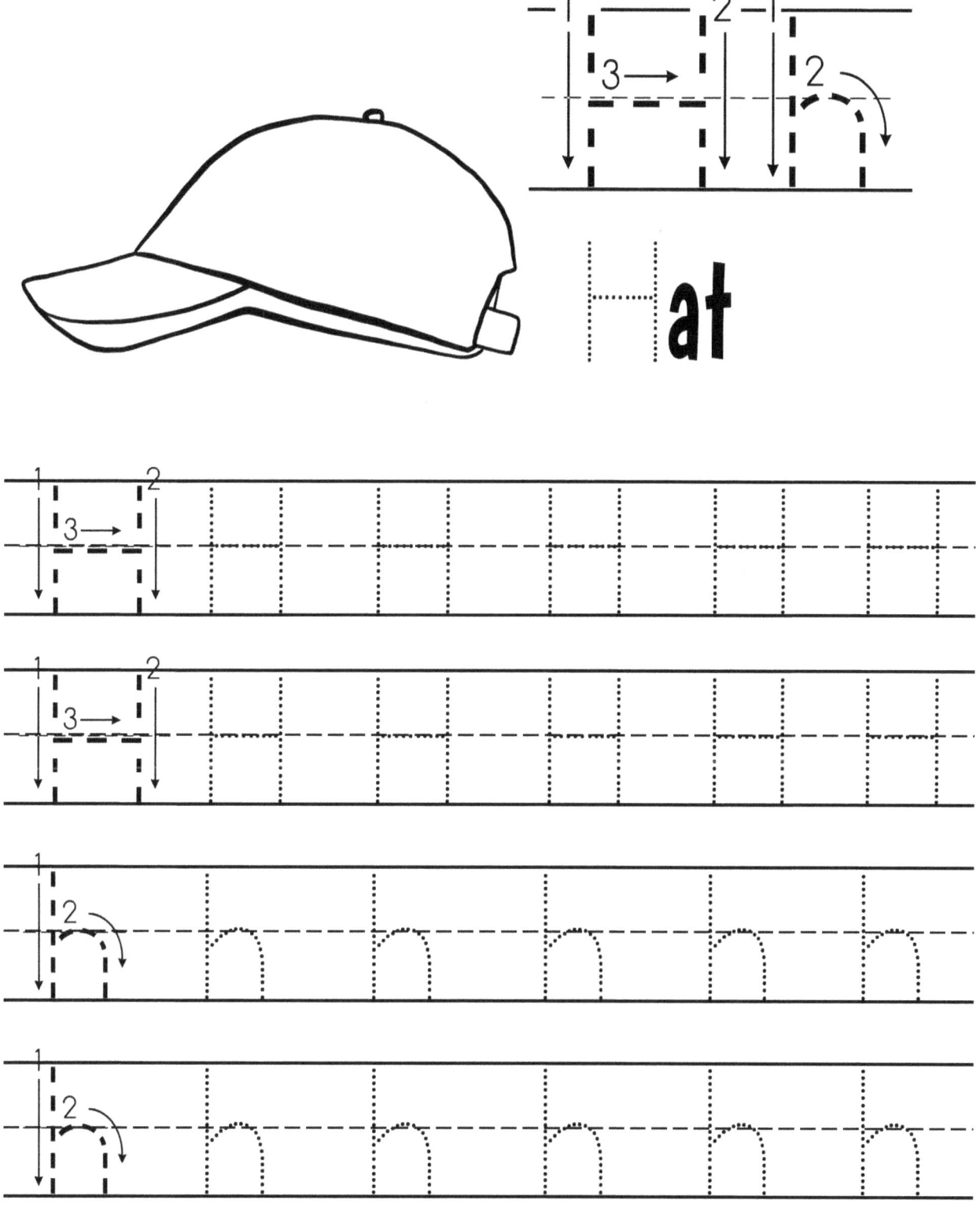

Ice cream

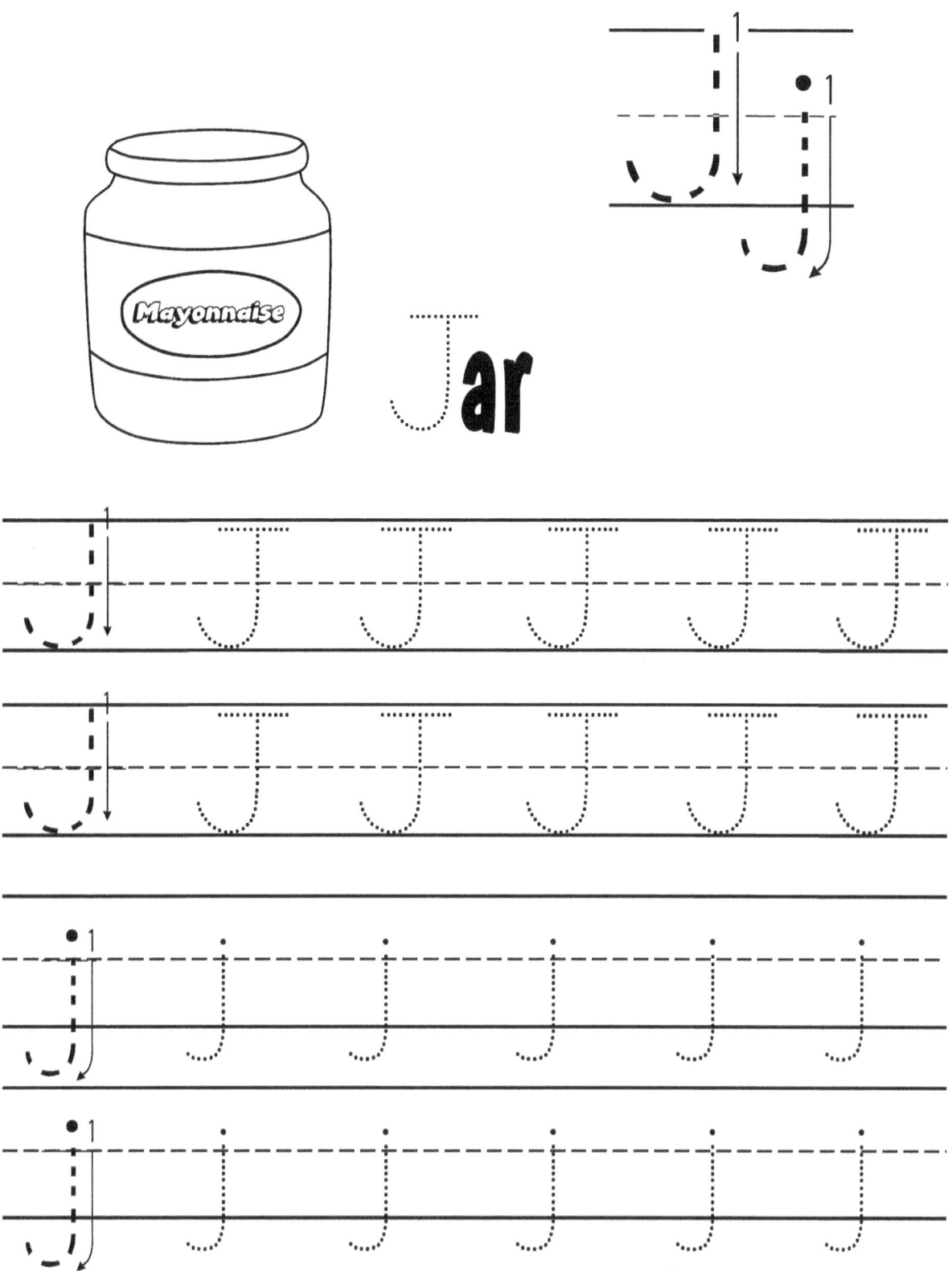

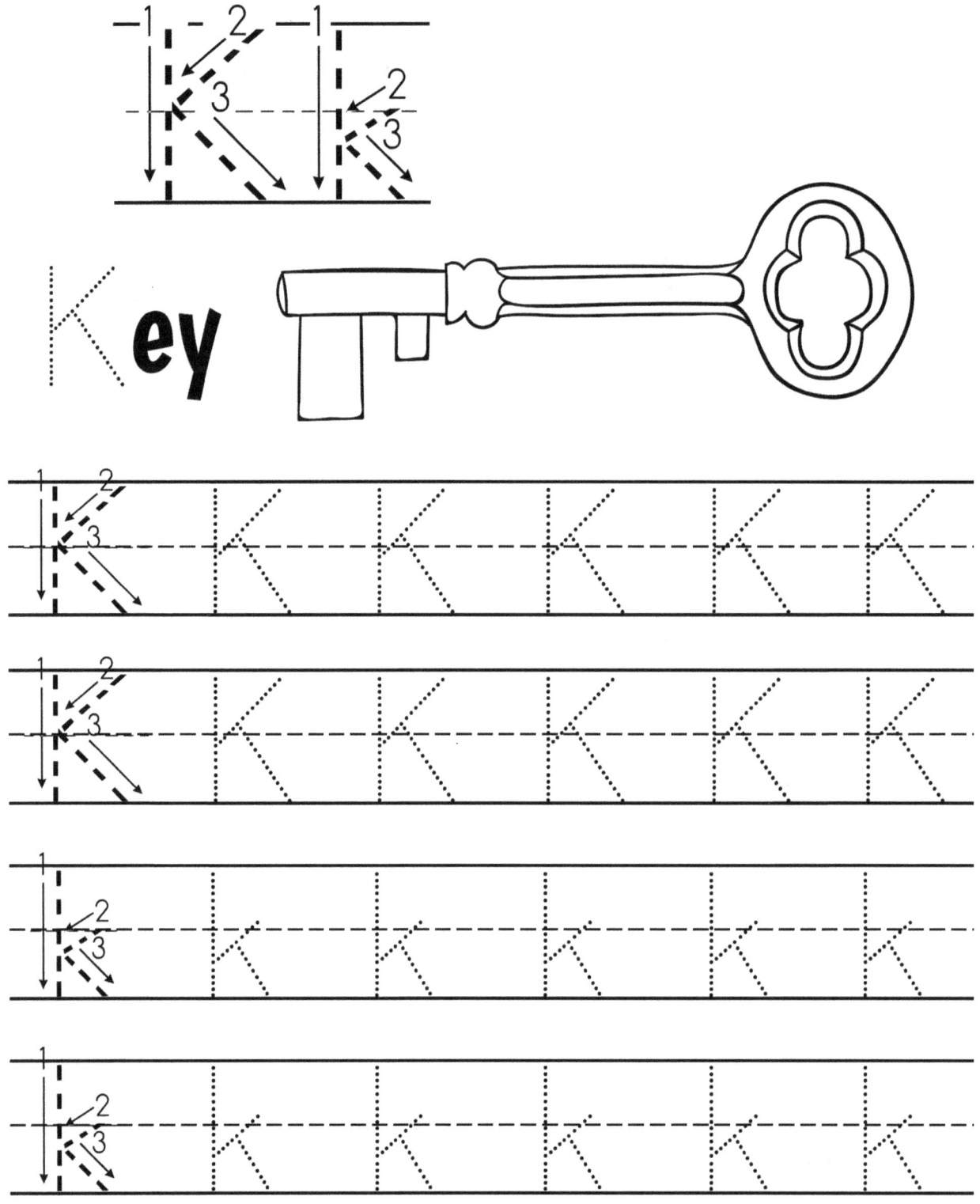

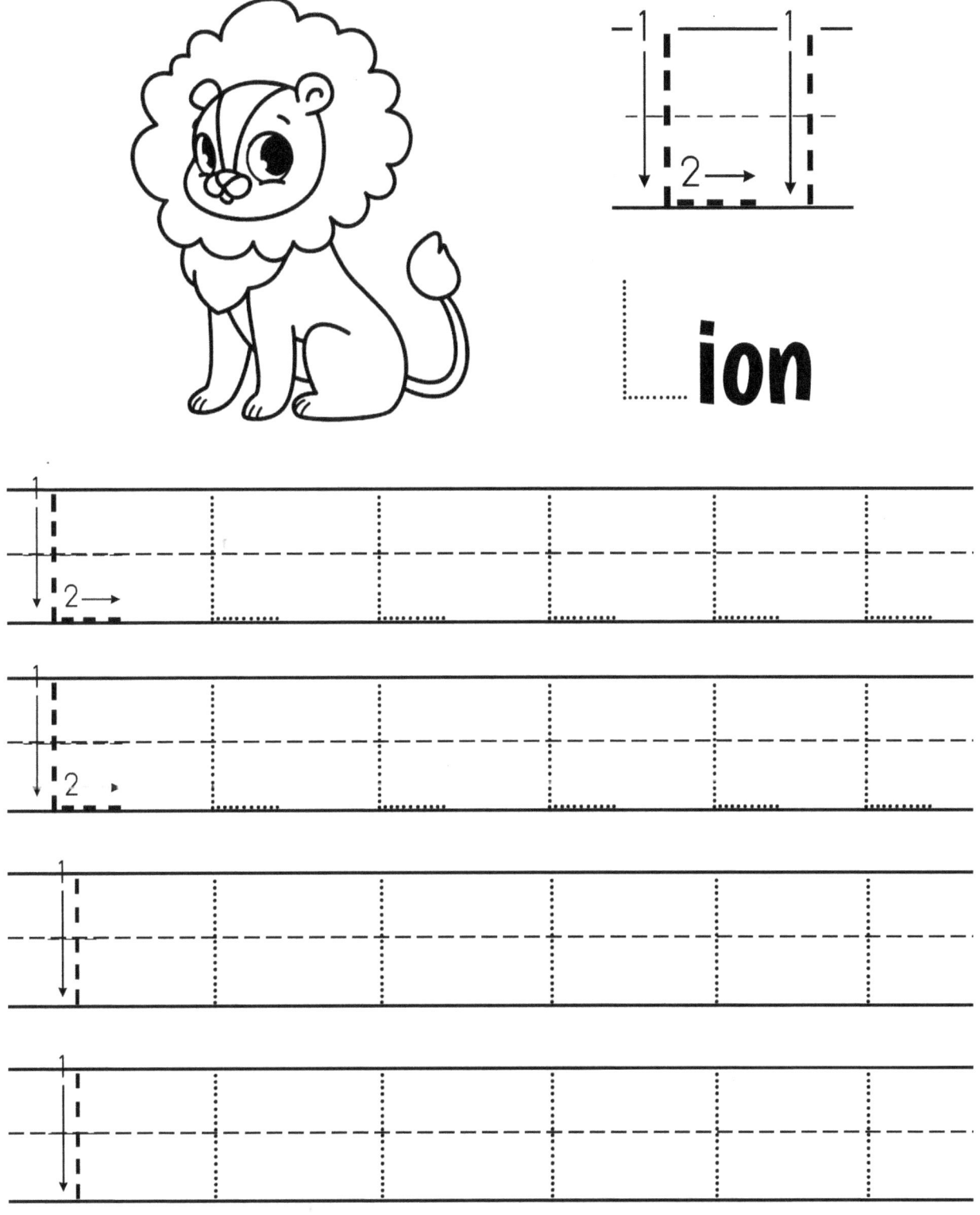

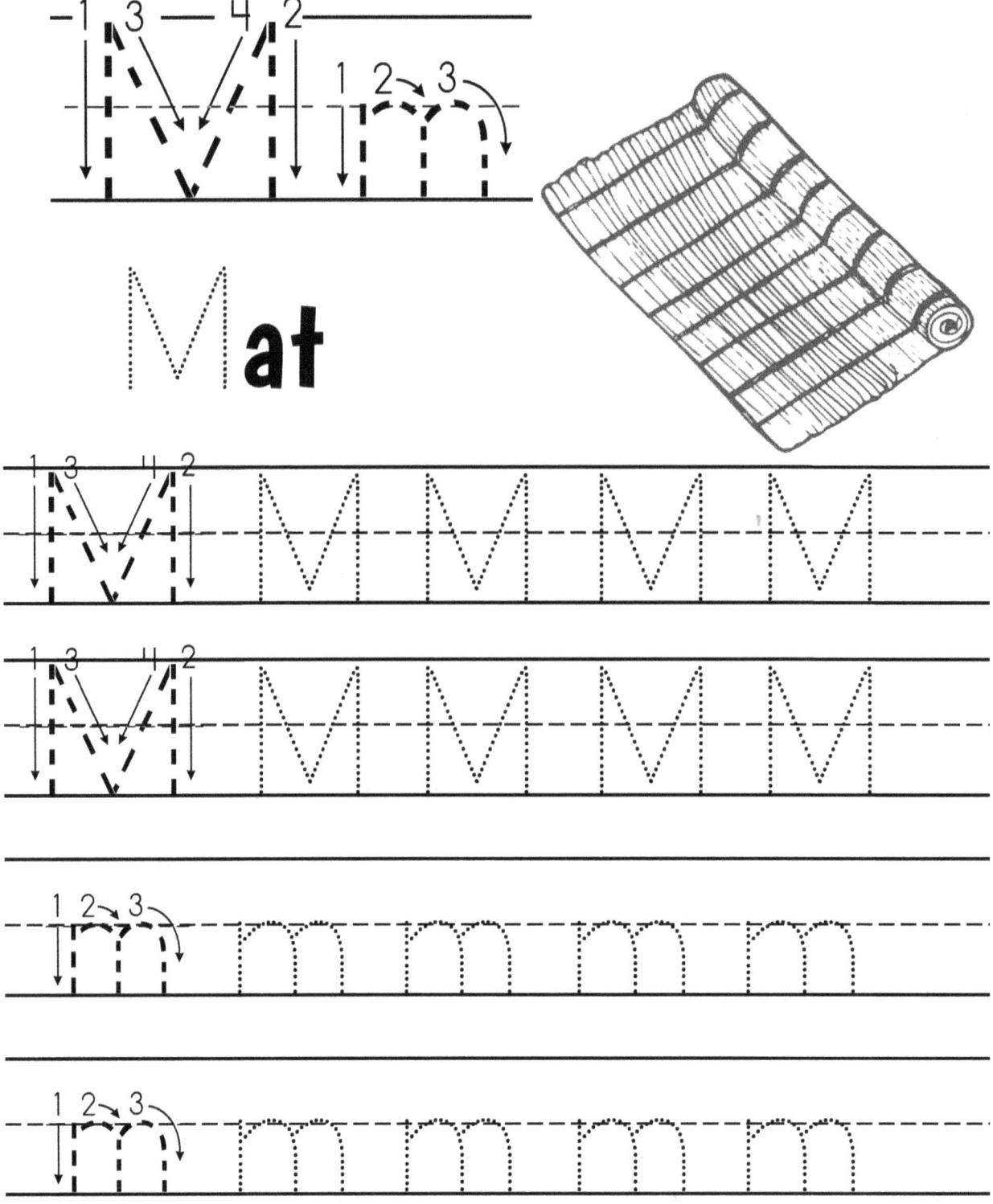

Mat

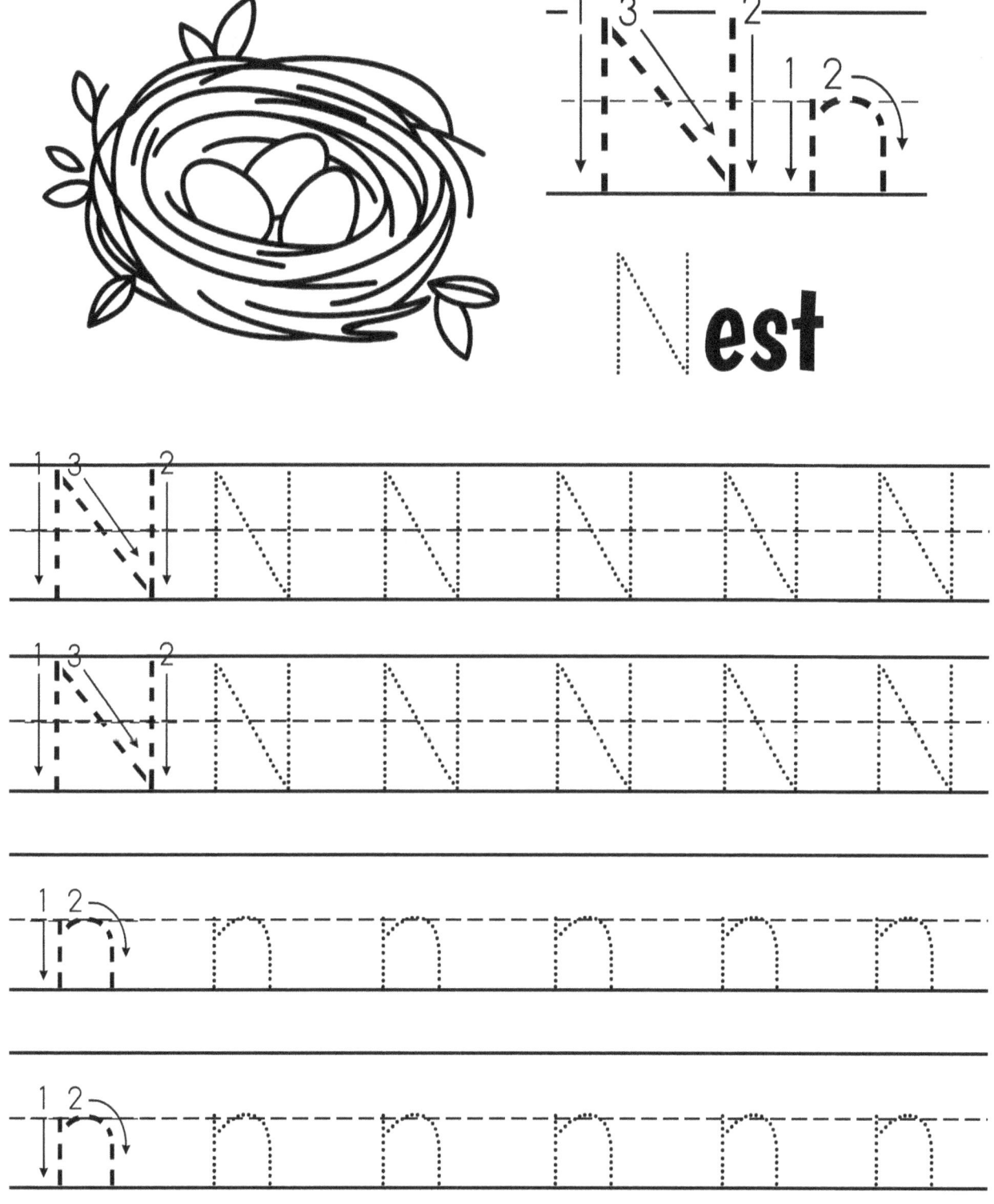

Nest

Owl

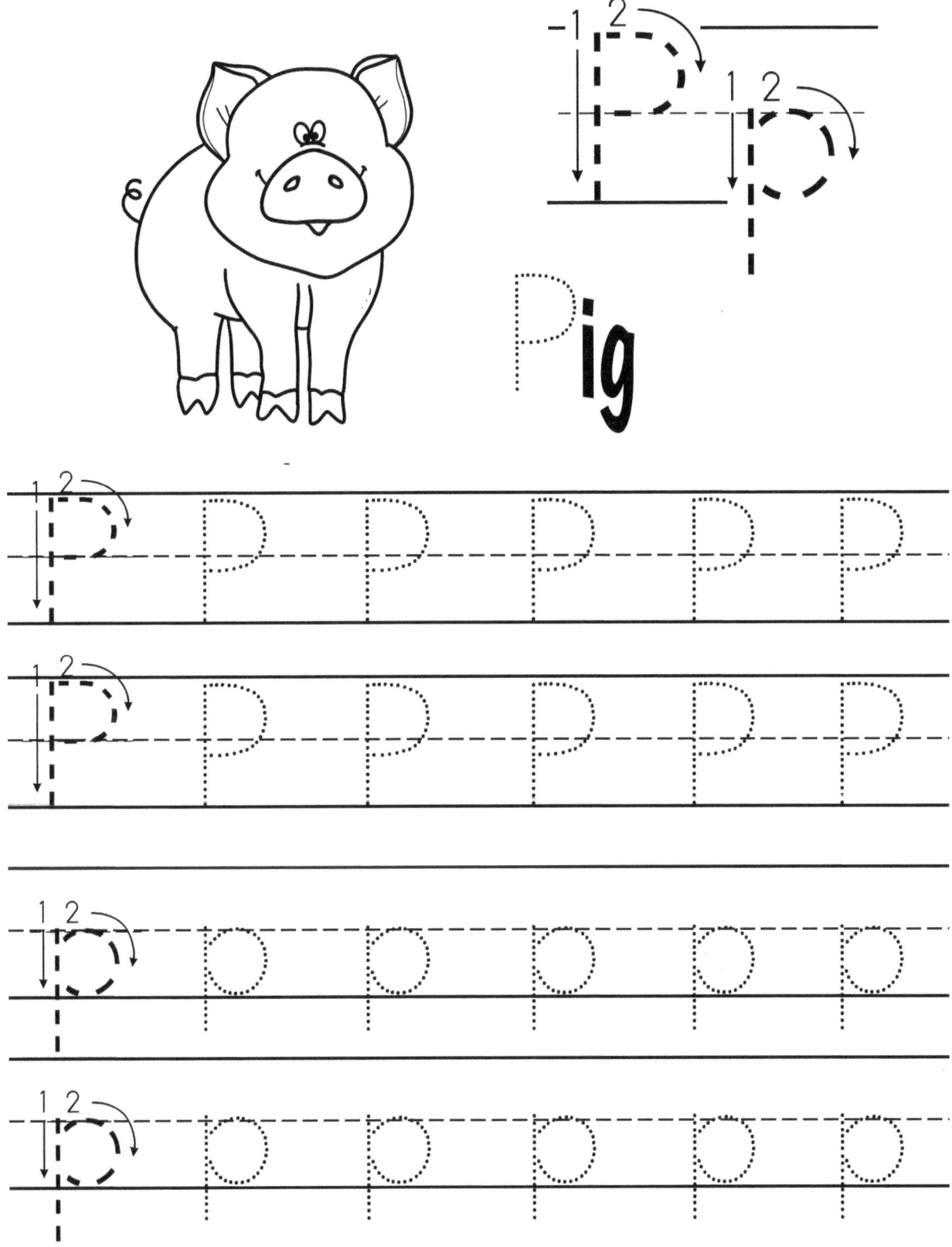

Queen

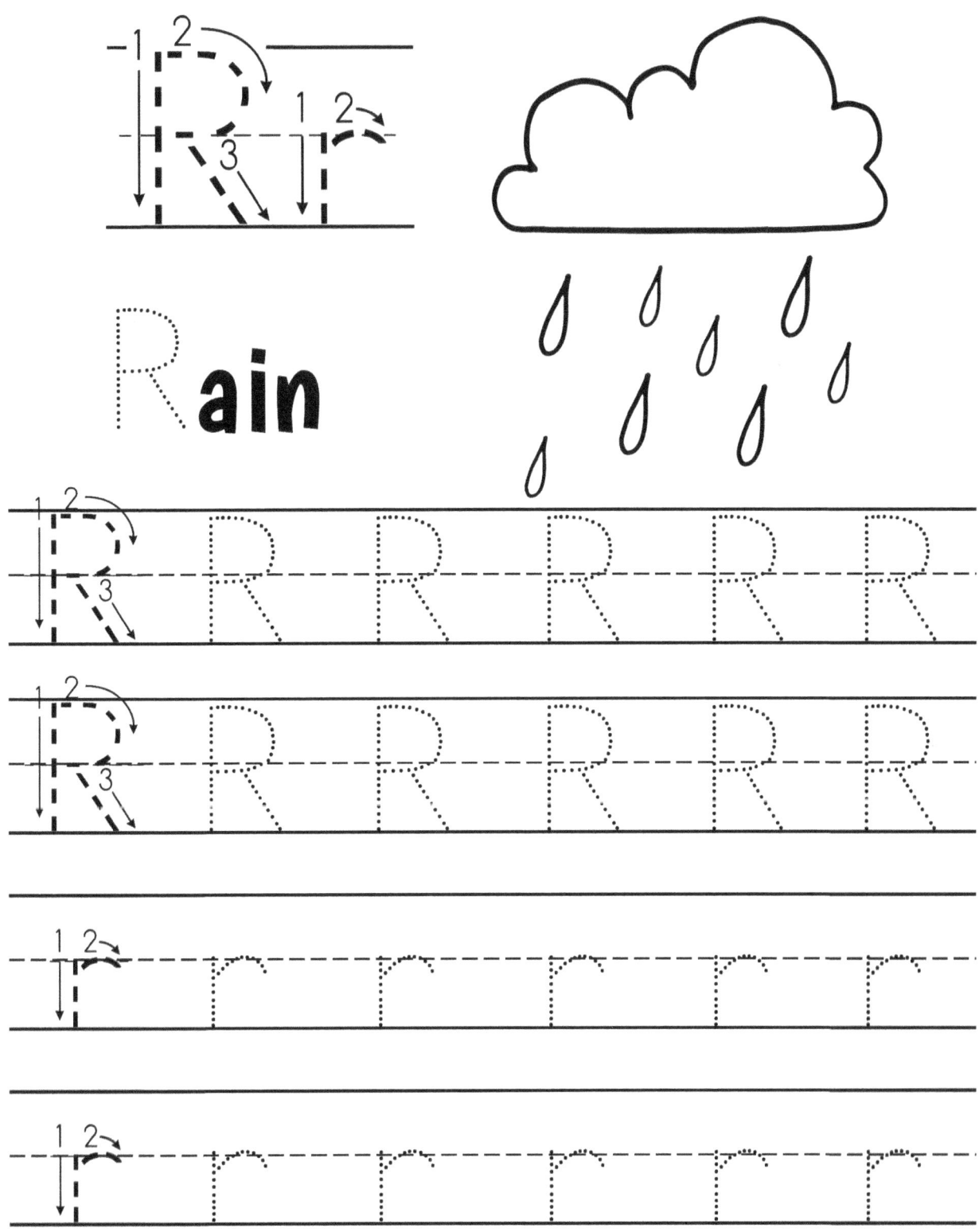

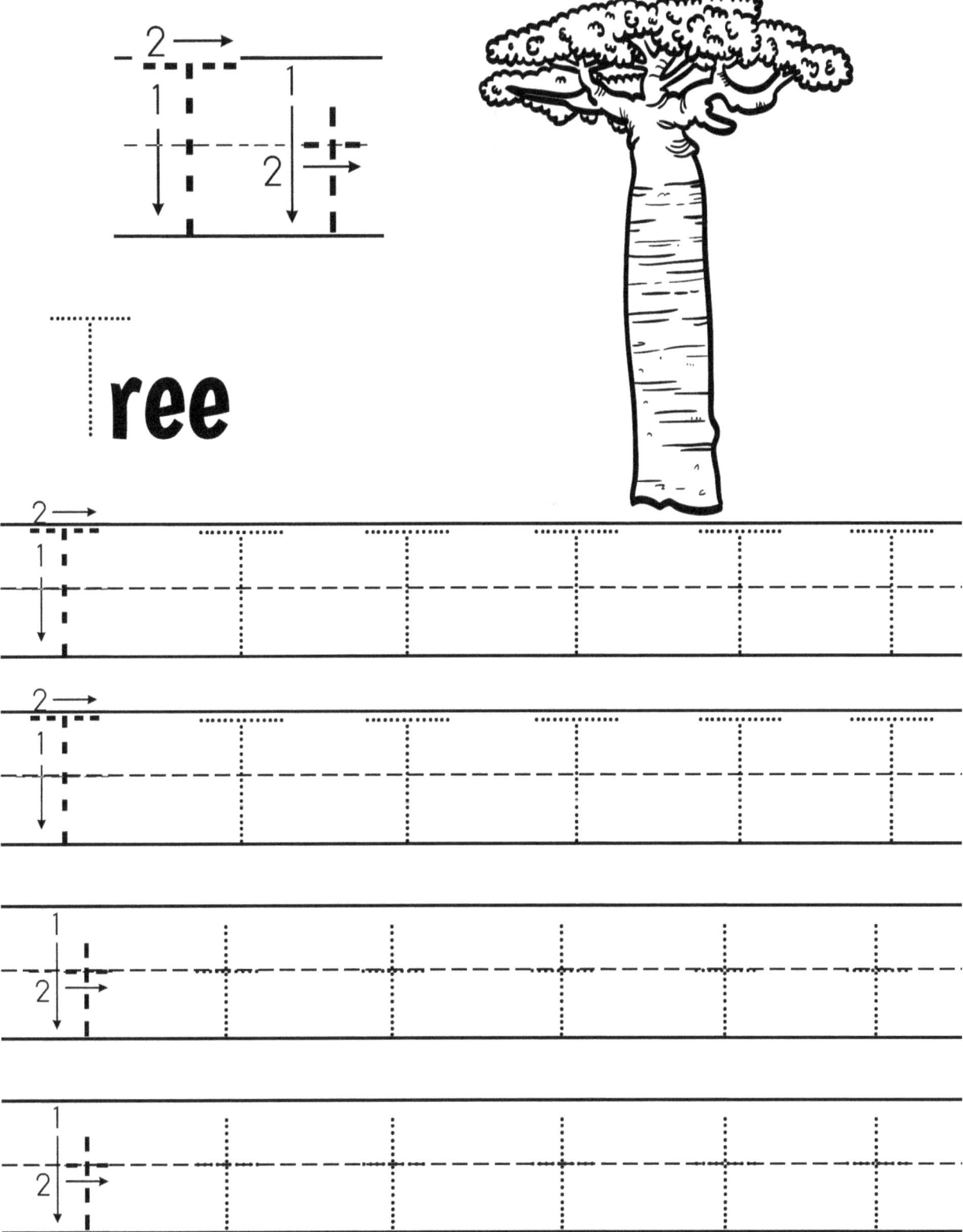

Tree

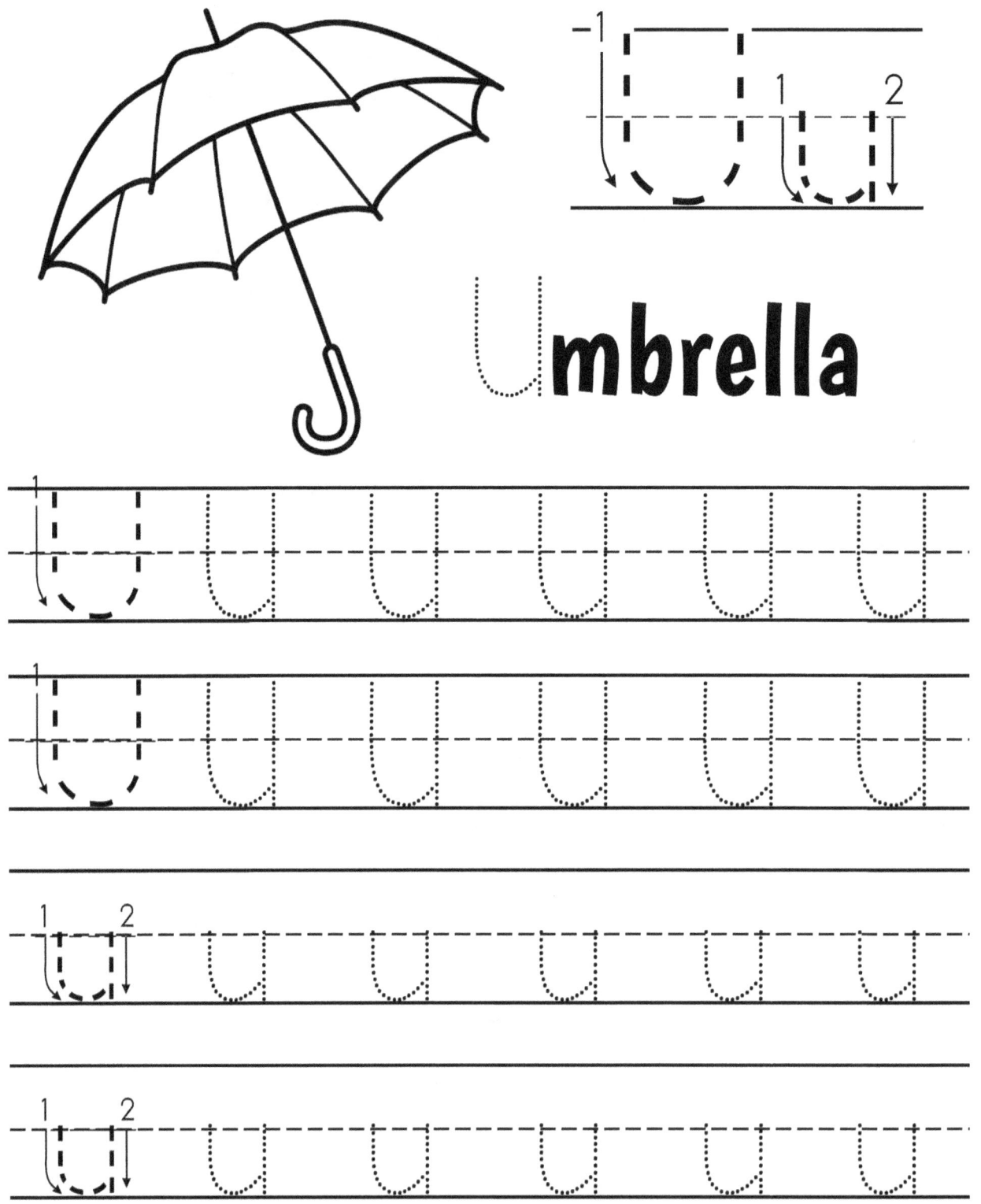

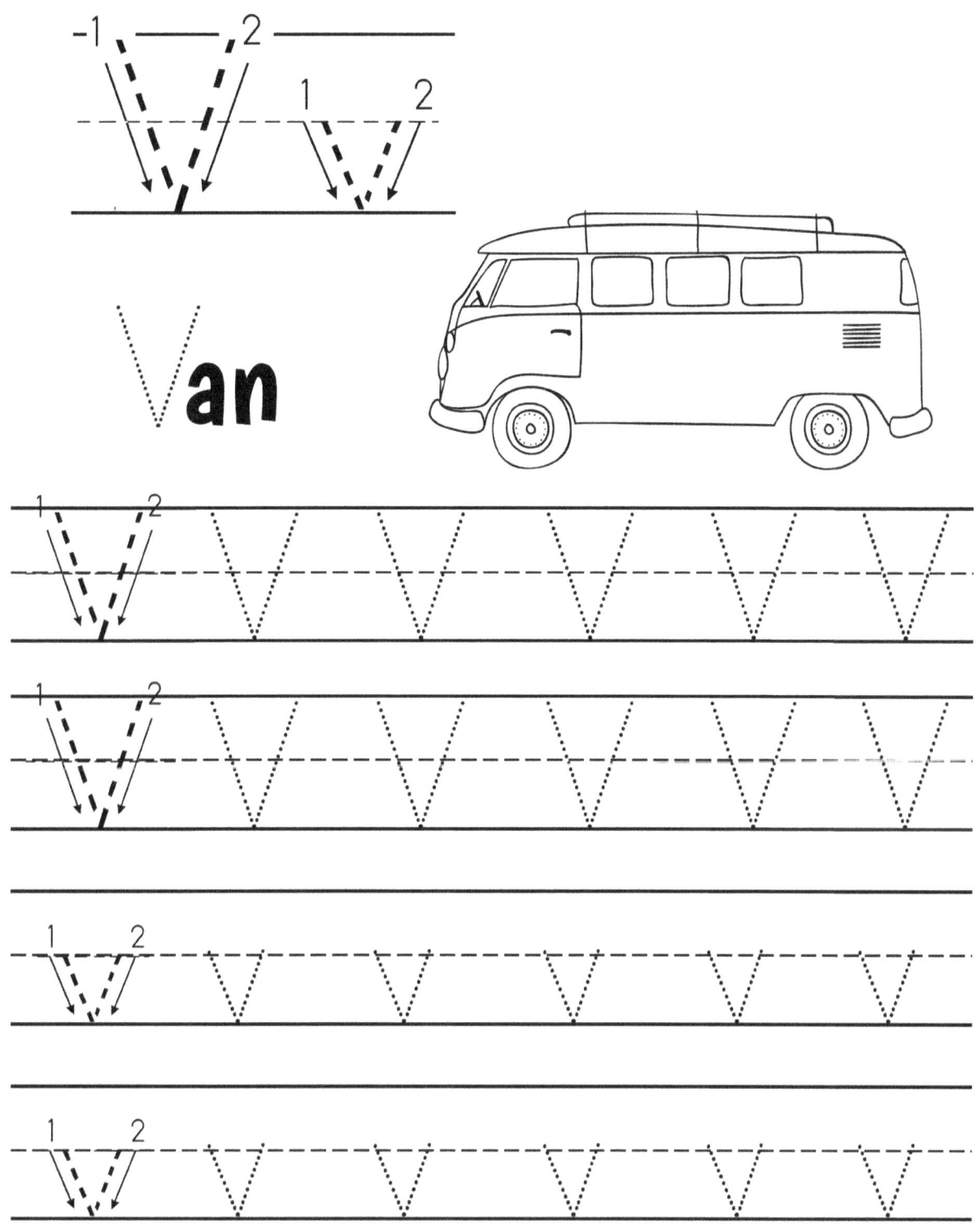

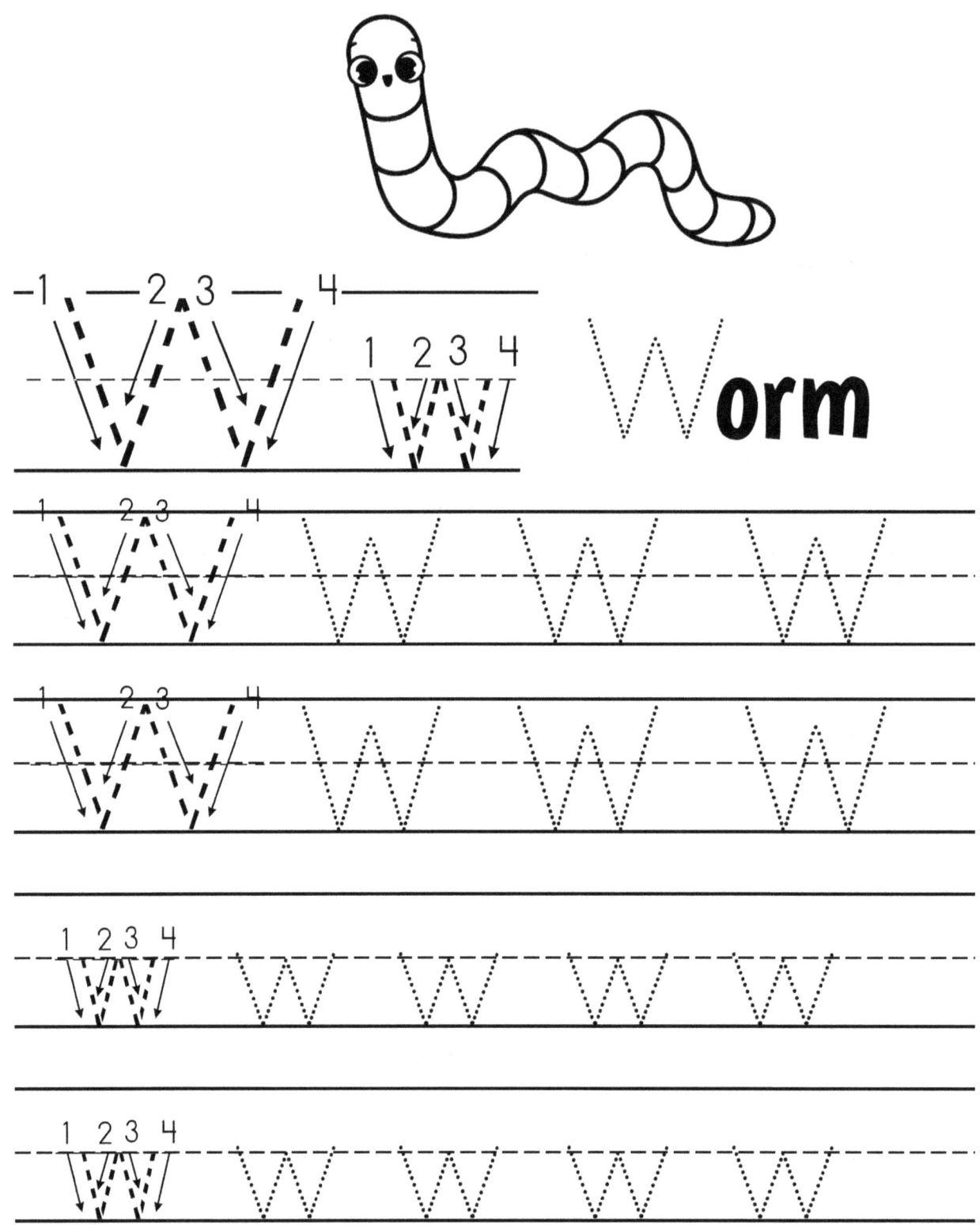

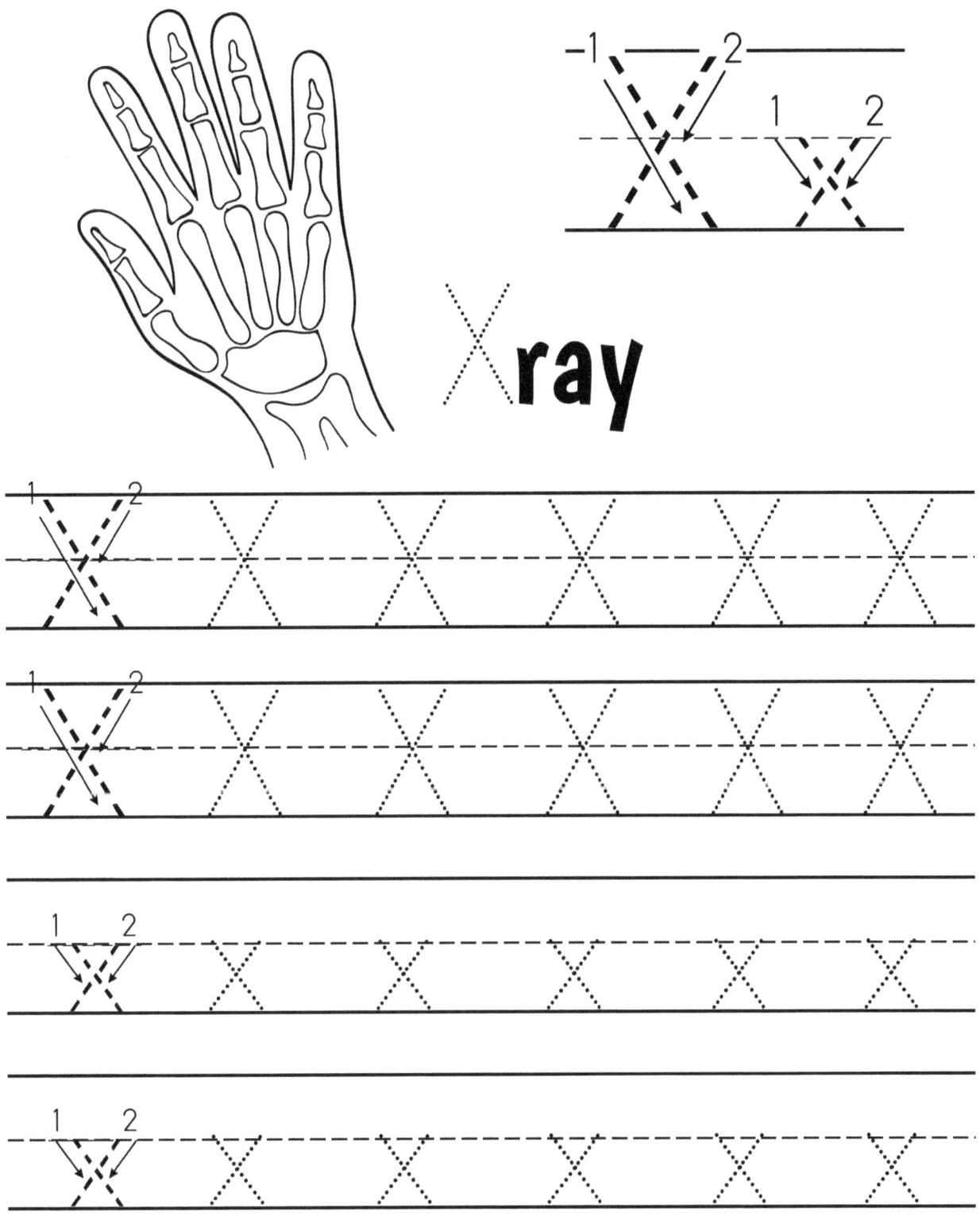

Xray

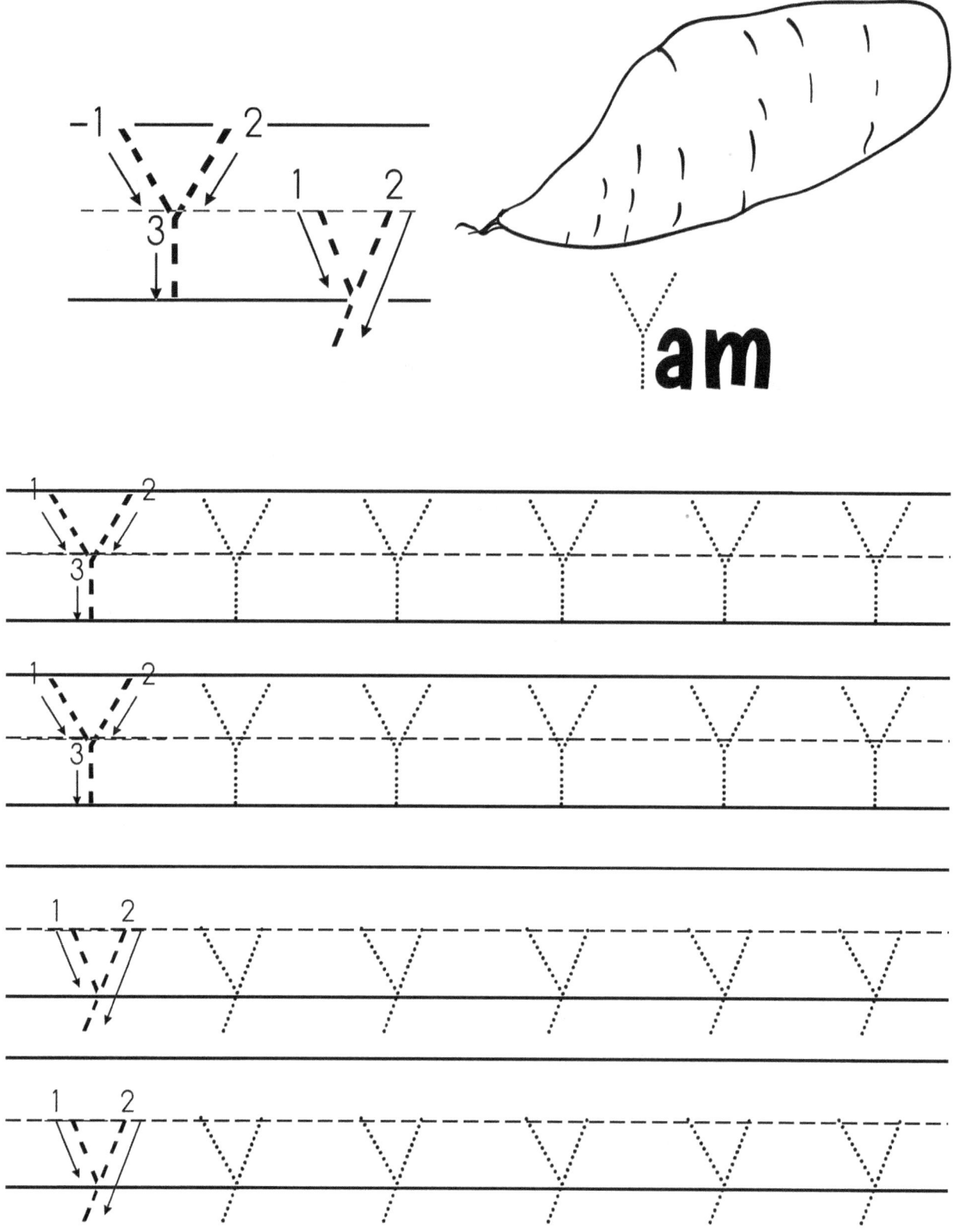

Yam

38

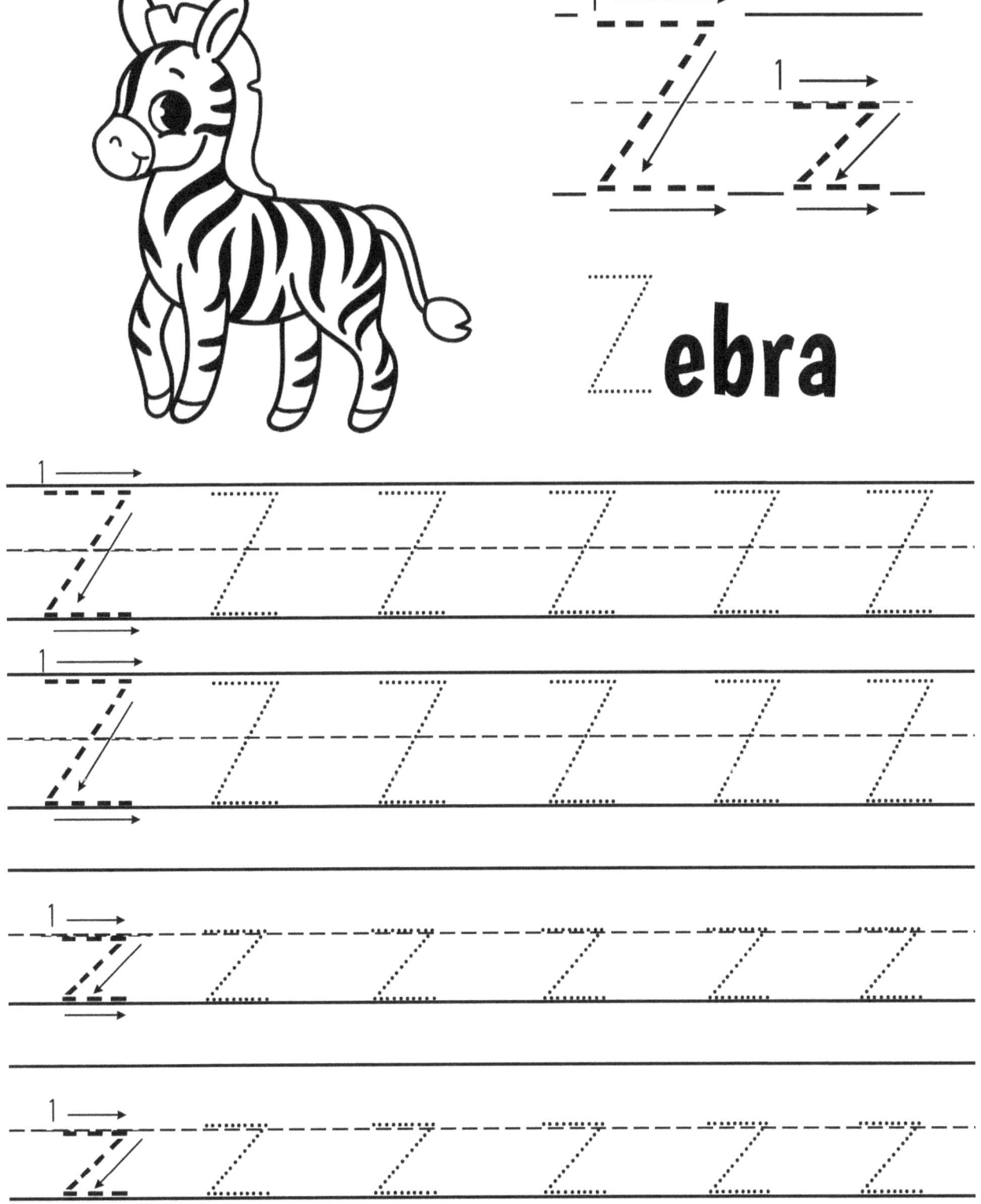

Zebra

Trace the Uppercase Letters

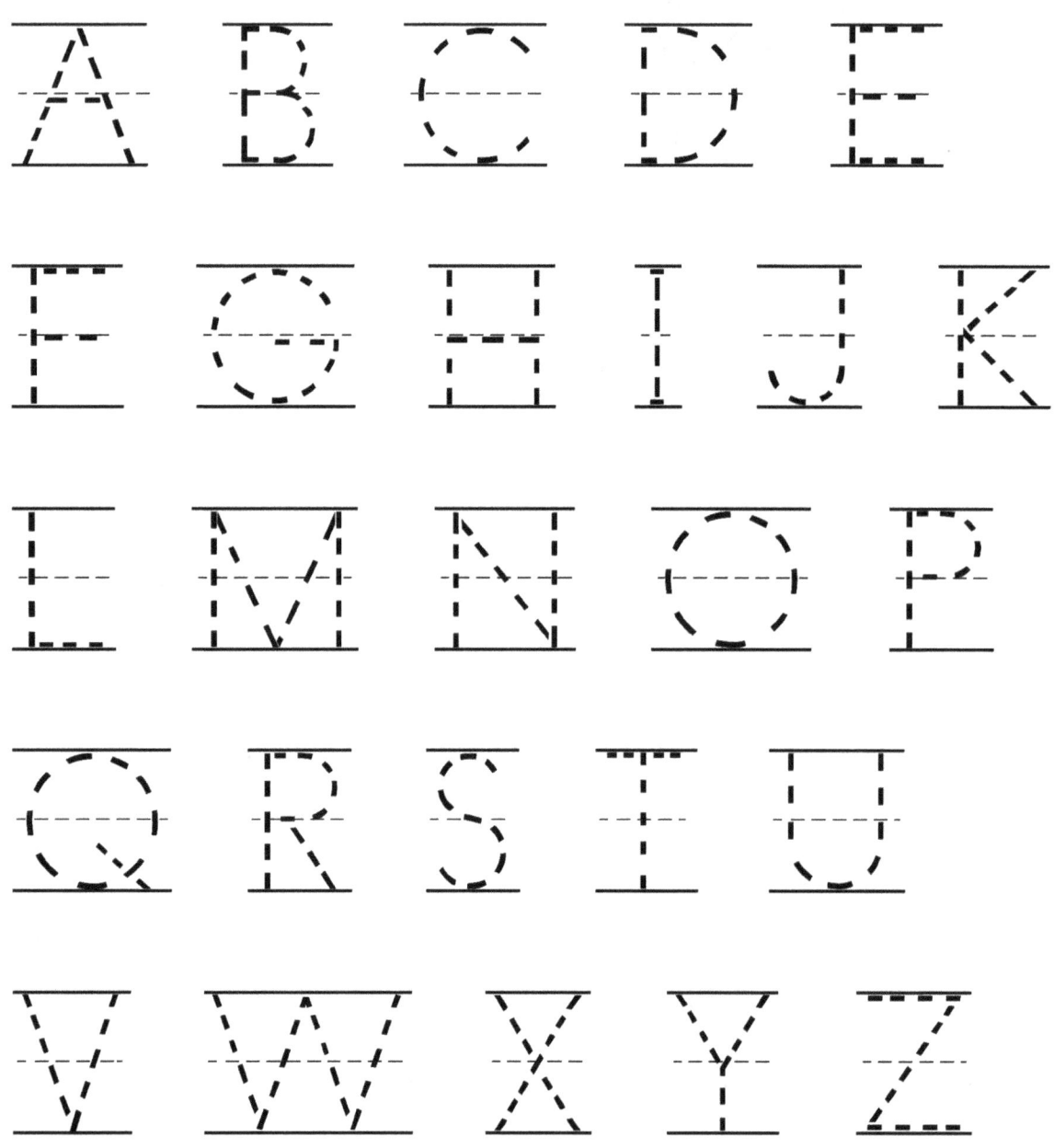

40

Trace the Lowercase Letters

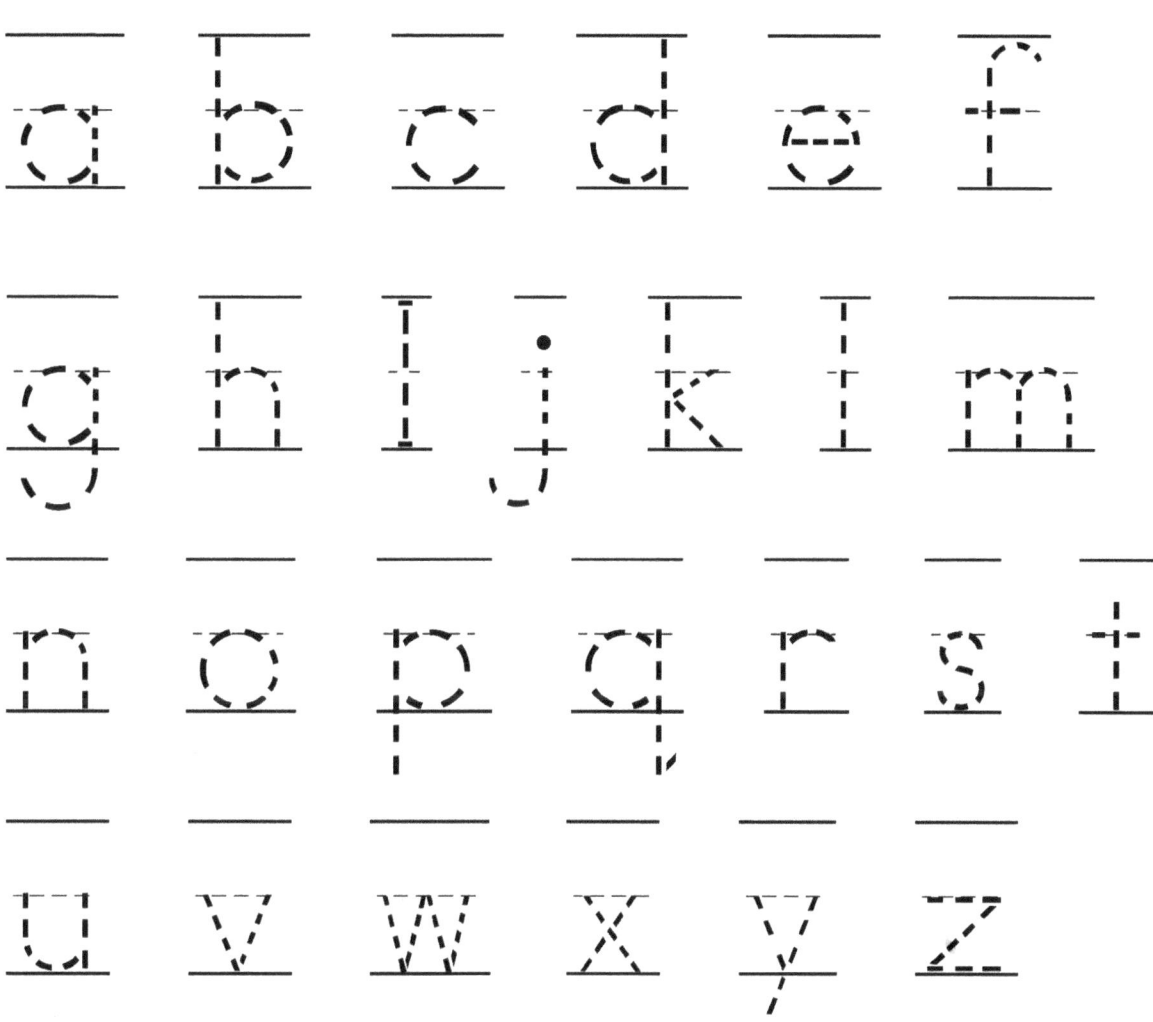

I Can Write My ABC's

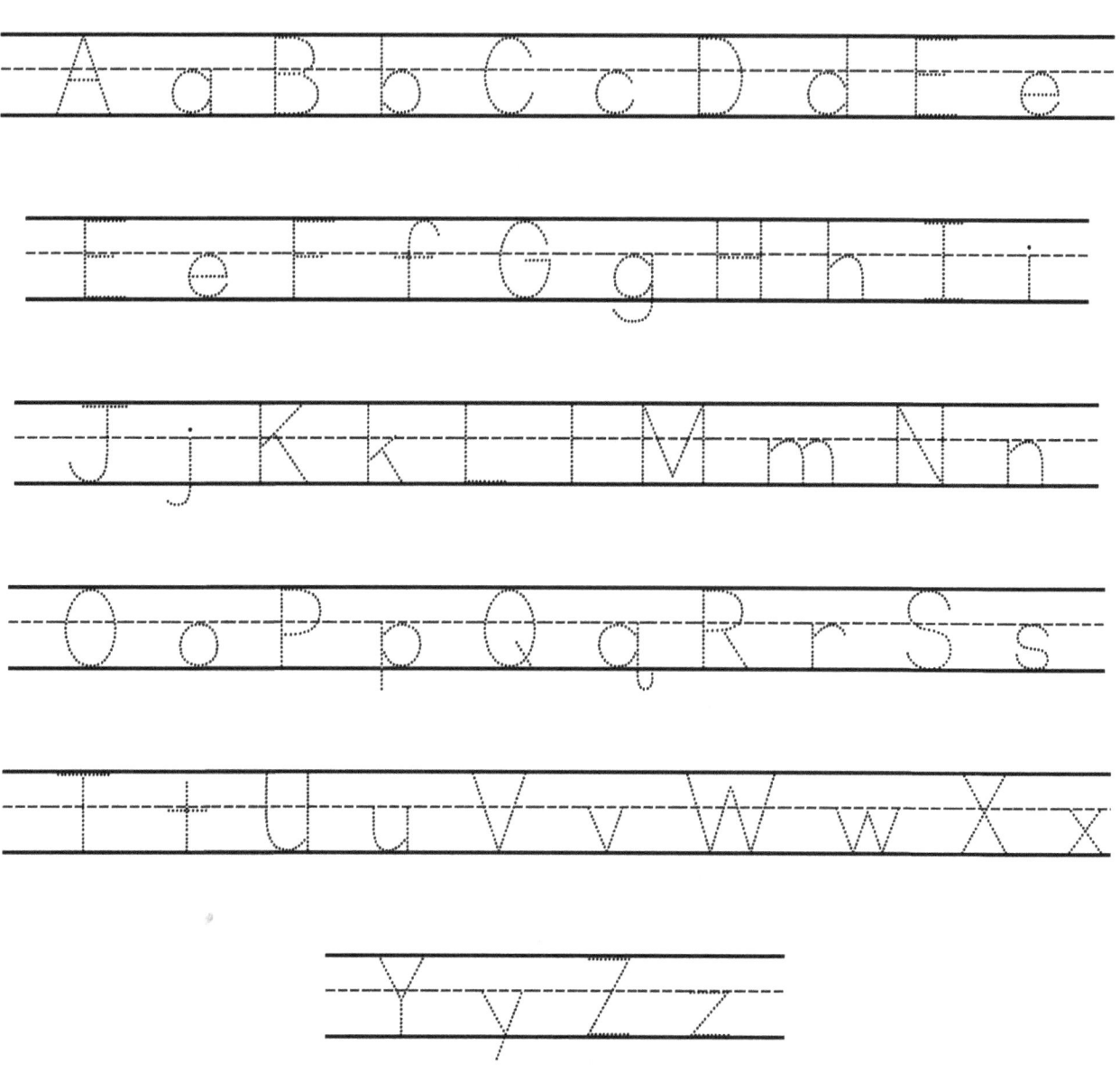

I Can Write My ABC's

I Can Write My ABC's

I Can Write My ABC's

I Can Write My ABC's

I Can Write My ABC's

I can learn to spell my First Name

I can learn to spell my Last Name

I can write my First Name

I can write my Last Name

I can write my First and Last Name

Name: ....

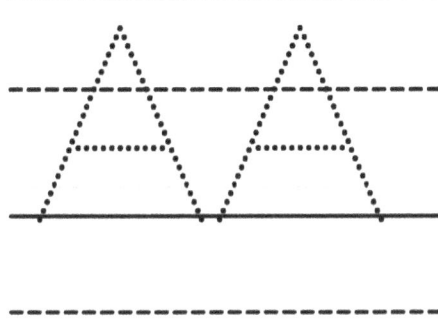

Find the Letters

Trace the letters. Then color the circles that have the letter you traced.

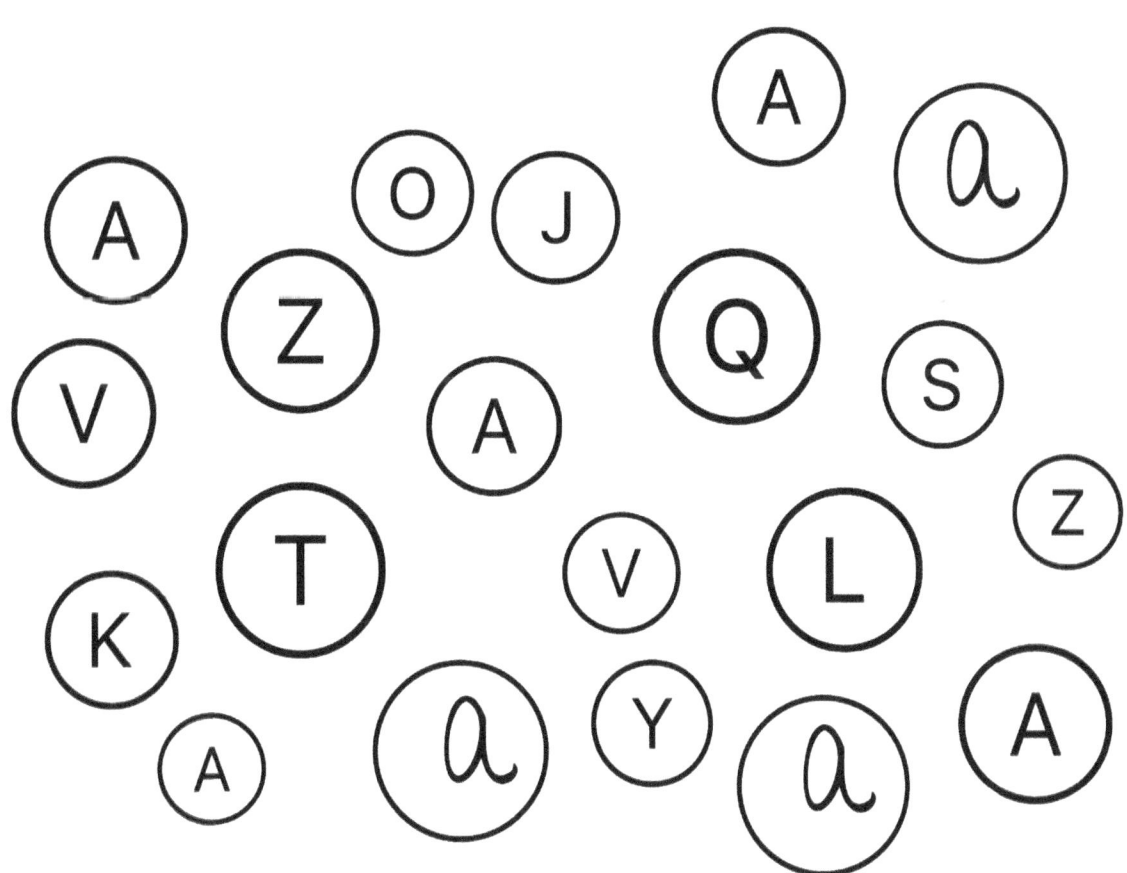

Name: _____

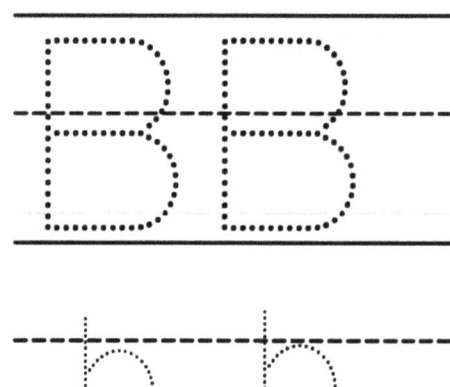

Find the letters

Trace the letters. Then color the circles that have the letter you traced.

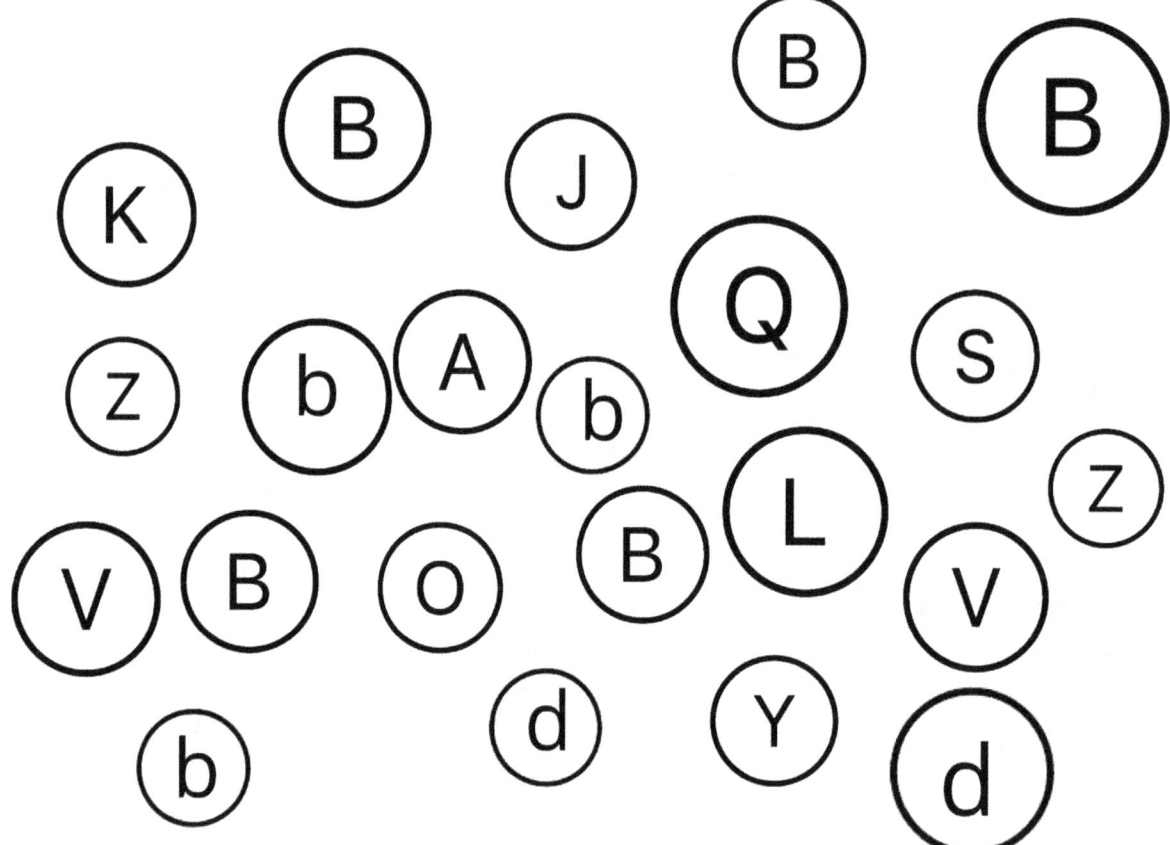

Name:

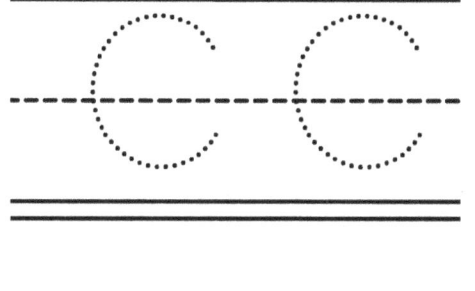

Find the Letters

Trace the letters. Then color the circles that have the letter you traced.

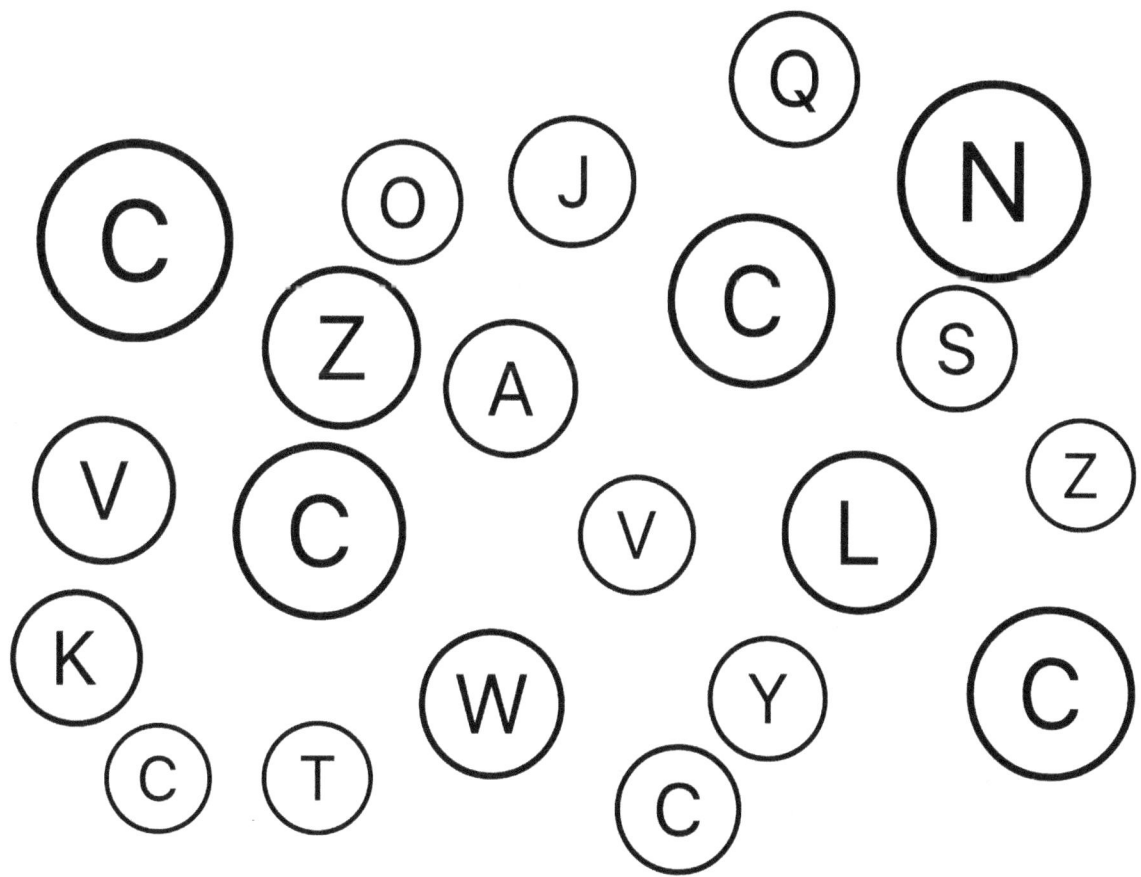

Name: ....

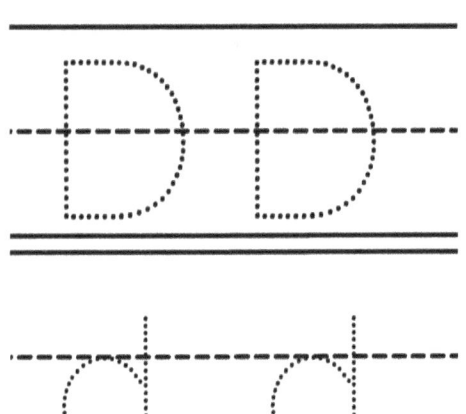

Find the letters

Trace the letters. Then color the circles that have the letter you traced.

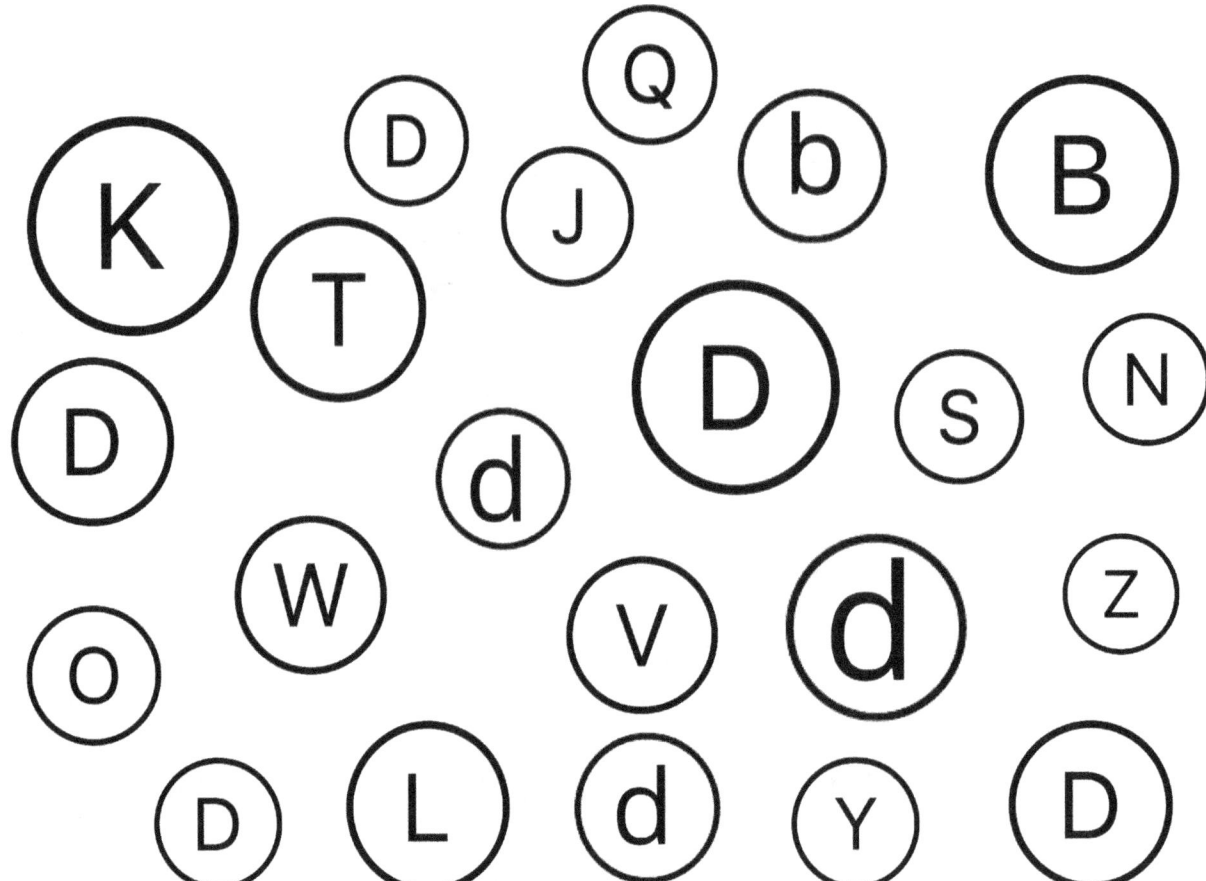

Name:

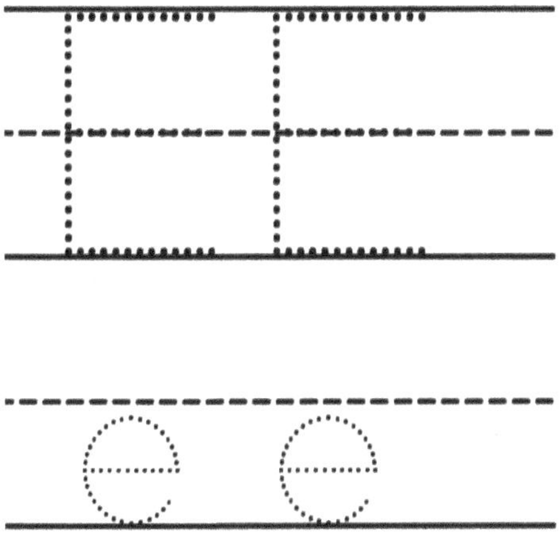

Find the Letters

Trace the letters. Then color the circles that have the letter you traced.

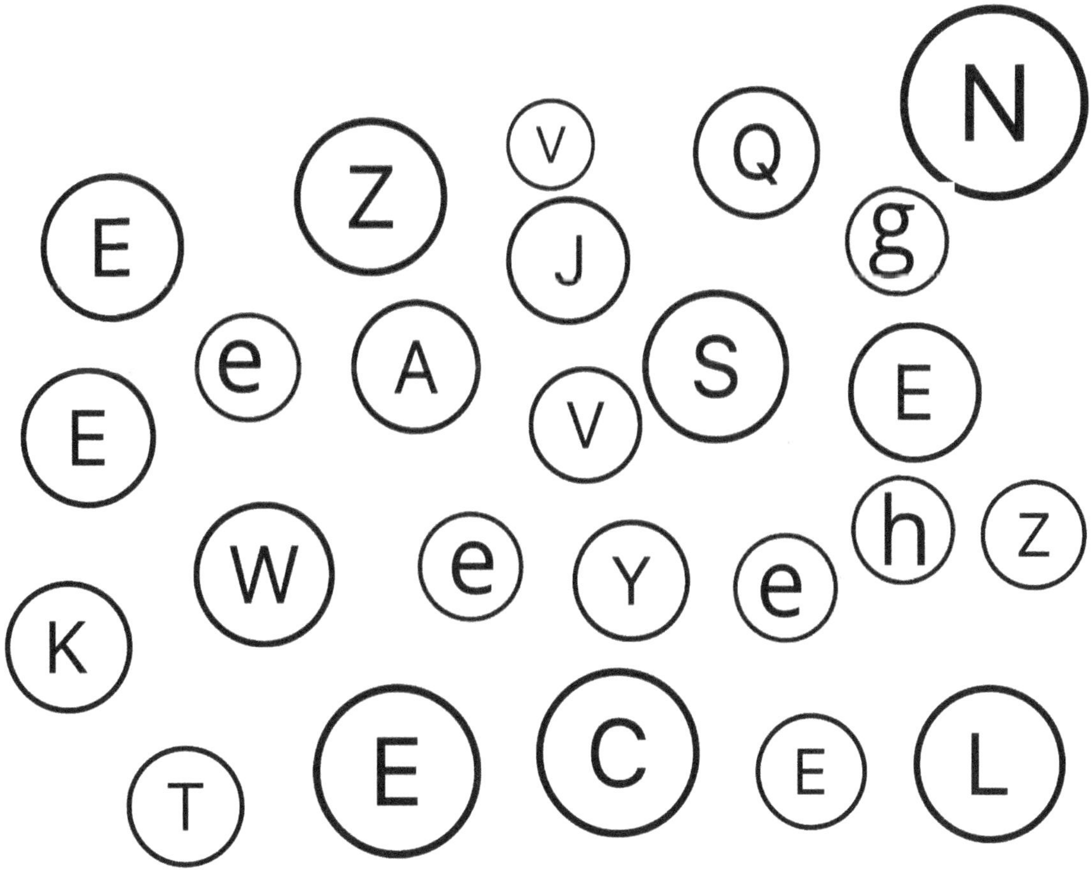

Name: ....

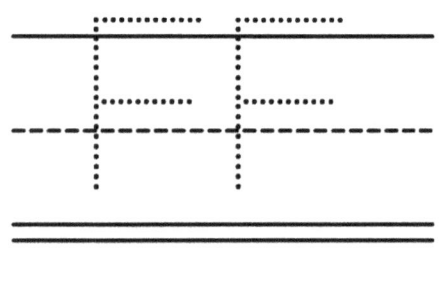

Find the letters

Trace the letters. Then color the circles that have the letter you traced.

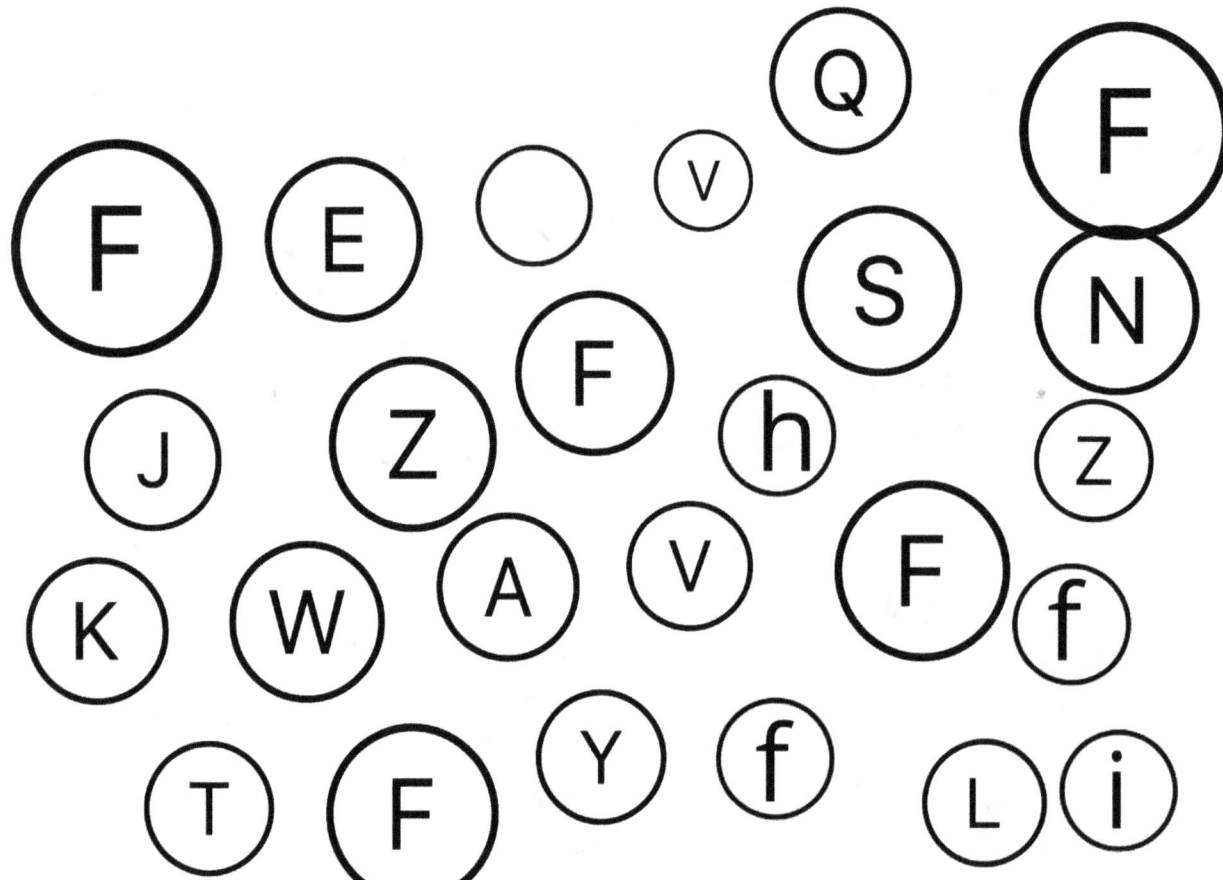

Name:

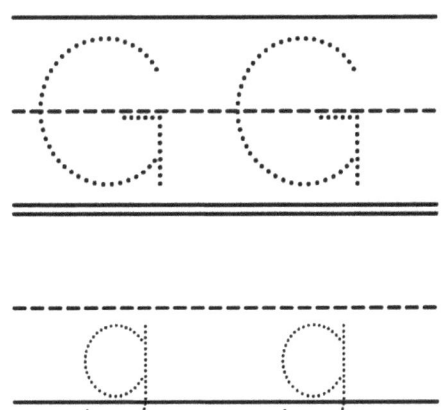

Find the Letters

Trace the letters. Then color the circles that have the letter you traced.

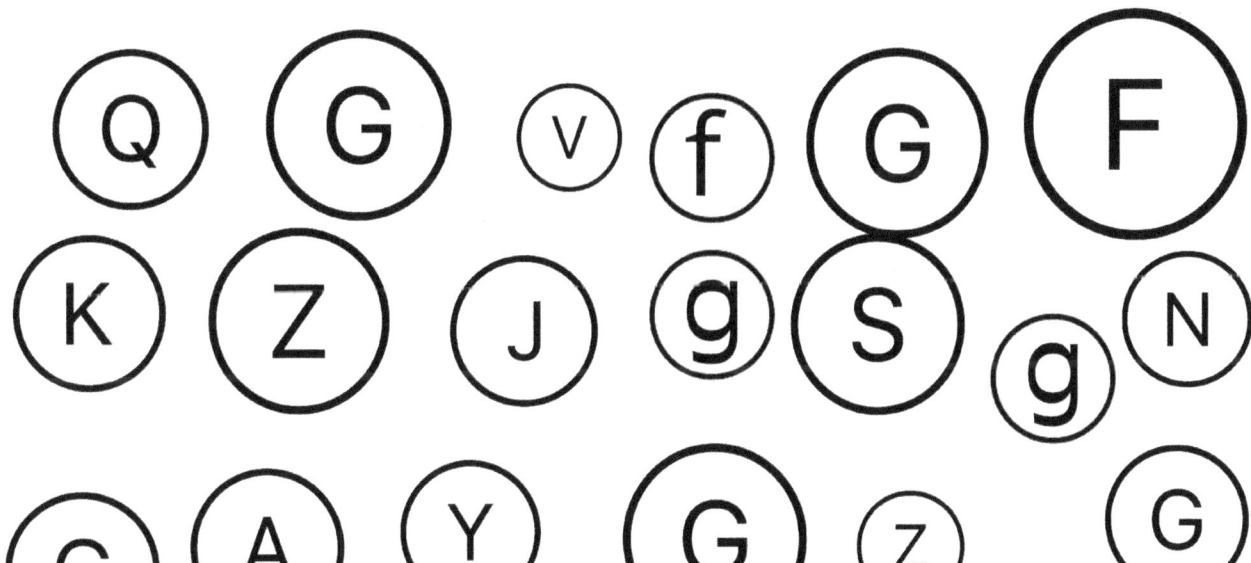

Name:

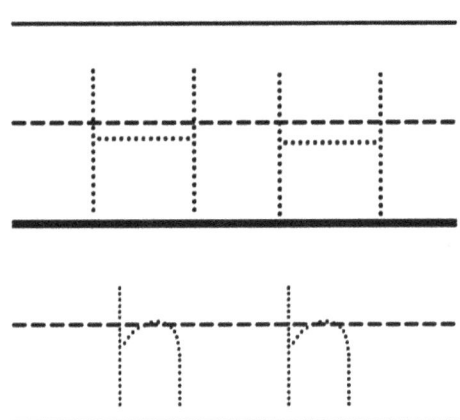

Find the letters

Trace the letters. Then color the circles that have the letter you traced.

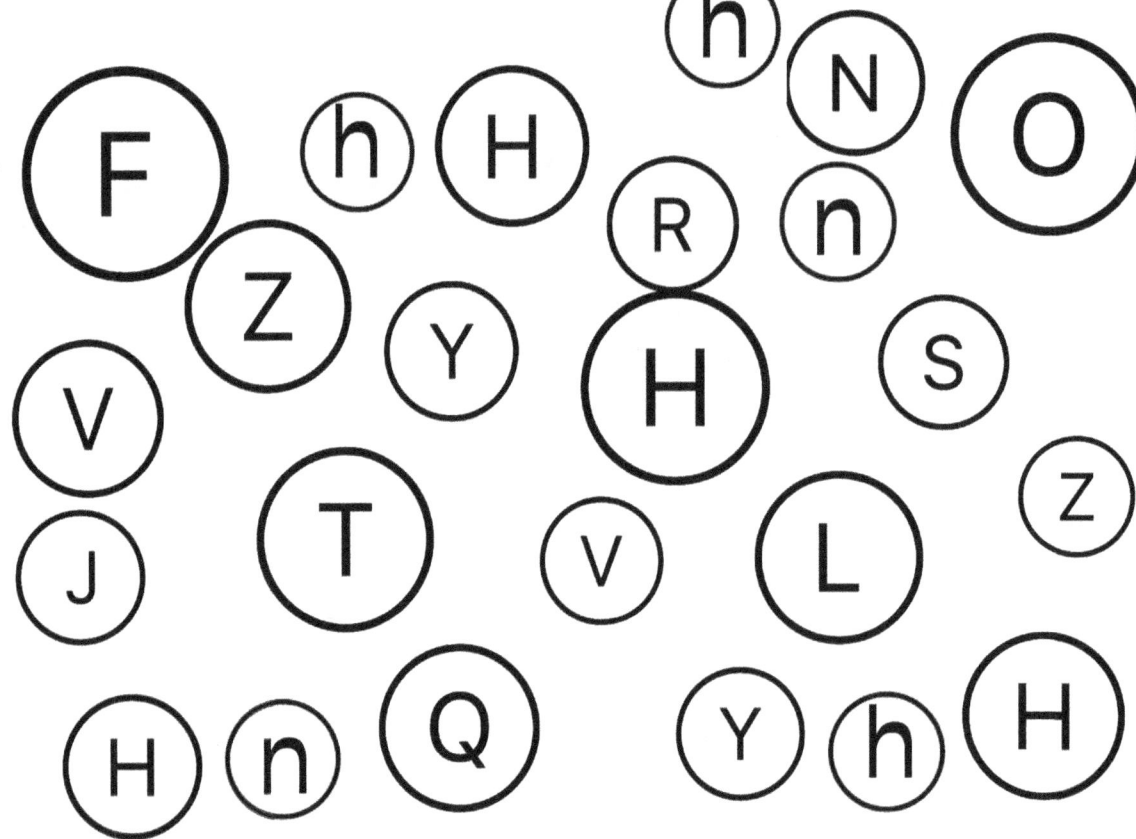

Name: ....

I i

Find the Letters
Trace the letters. Then color the circles that have the letter you traced.

(Z) (Z) (i) (N) (I)
(I)
(I) (Y) (R) (I) (S)
(T) (i) (i)
(J) (V) (L)
(V) (i) (Y) (Q)

Name:

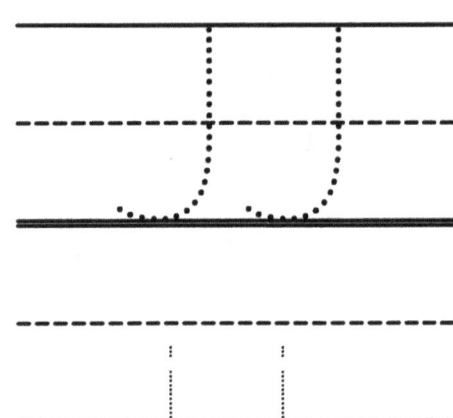

Find the letters

Trace the letters. Then color the circles that have the letter you traced.

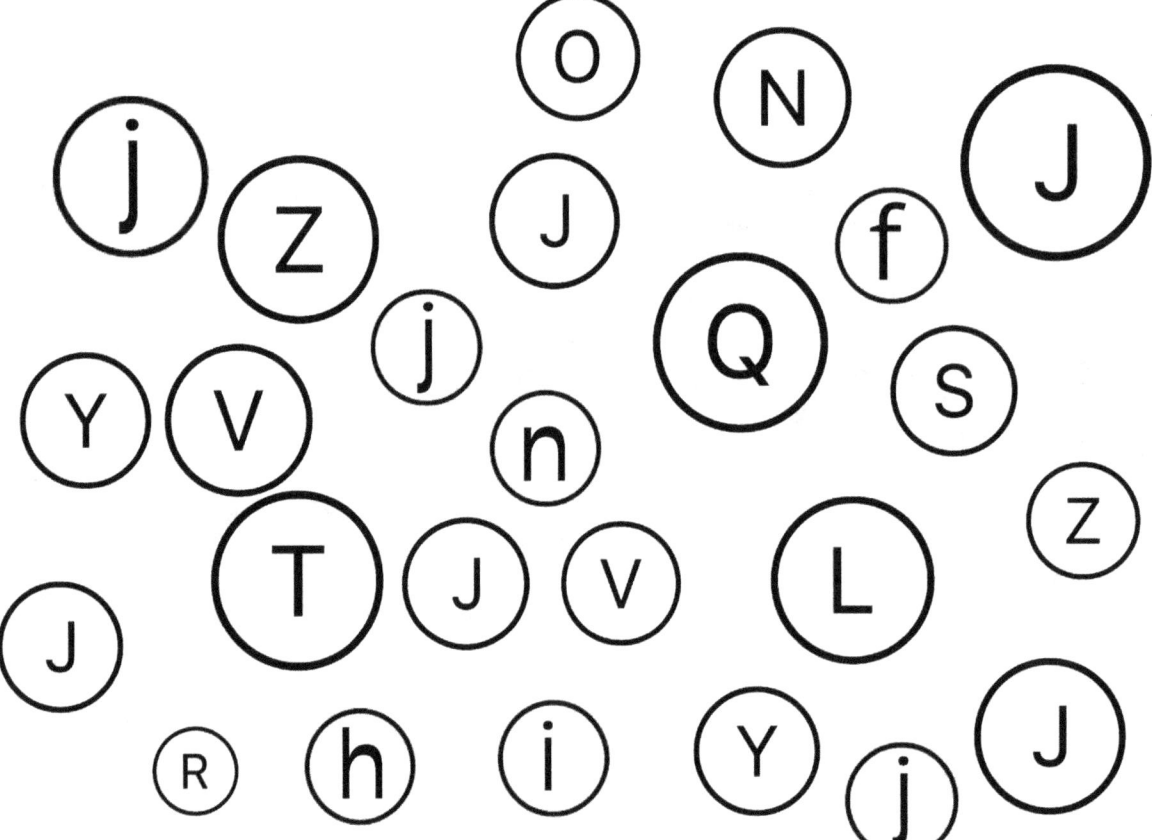

Name:

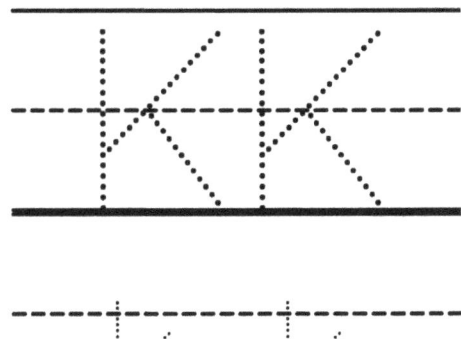

Find the Letters

Trace the letters. Then color the circles that have the letter you traced.

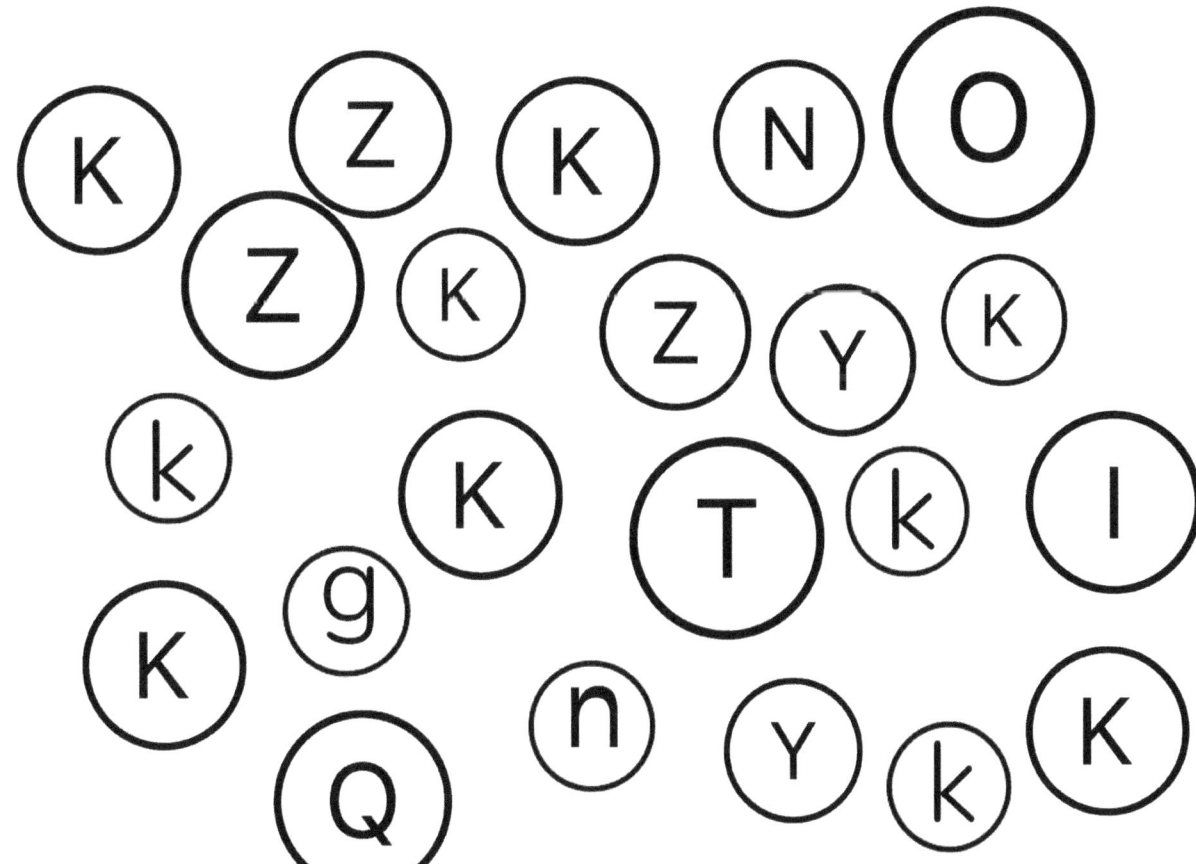

Name:

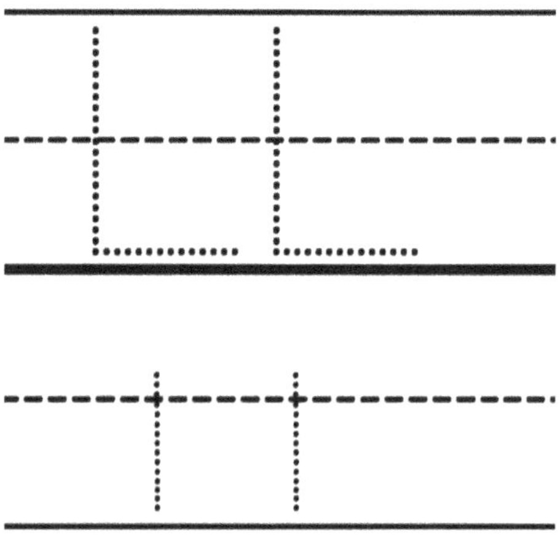

Find the letters

Trace the letters. Then color the circles that have the letter you traced.

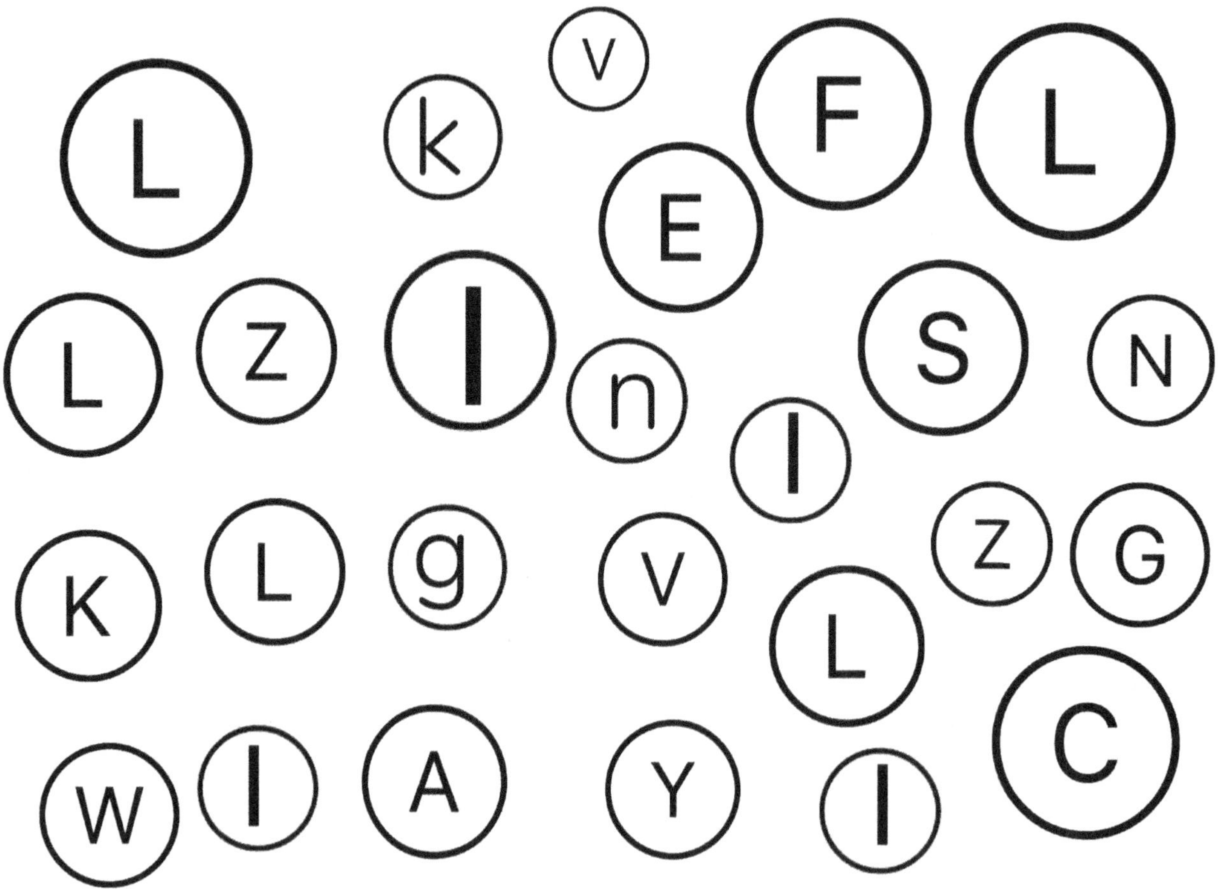

Name:

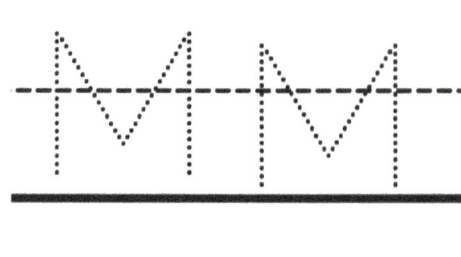

Find the Letters

Trace the letters. Then color the circles that have the letter you traced.

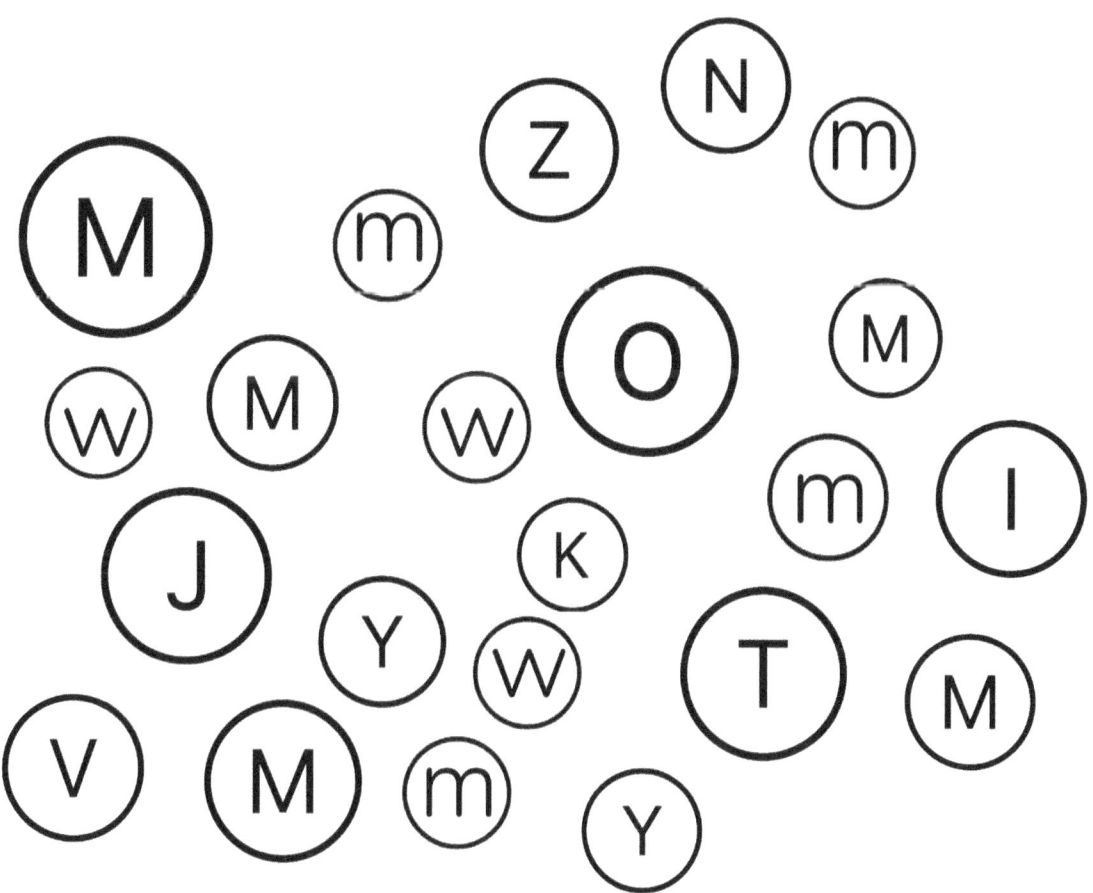

63

Name: ....

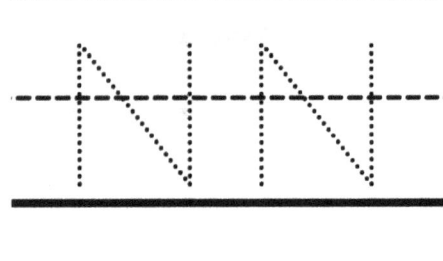

Find the letters

Trace the letters. Then color the circles that have the letter you traced.

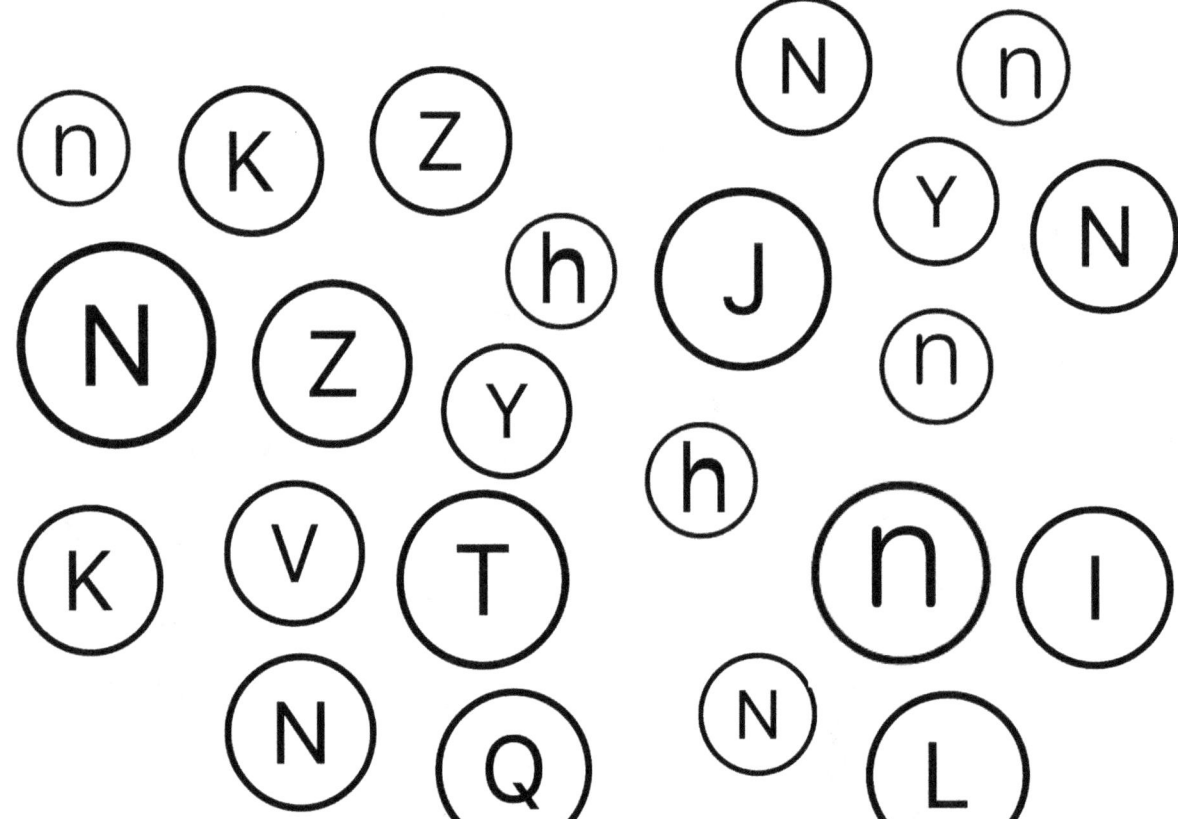

Name: ....

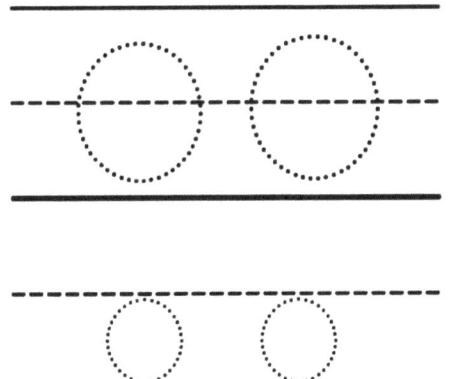

Find the Letters

Trace the letters. Then color the circles that have the letter you traced.

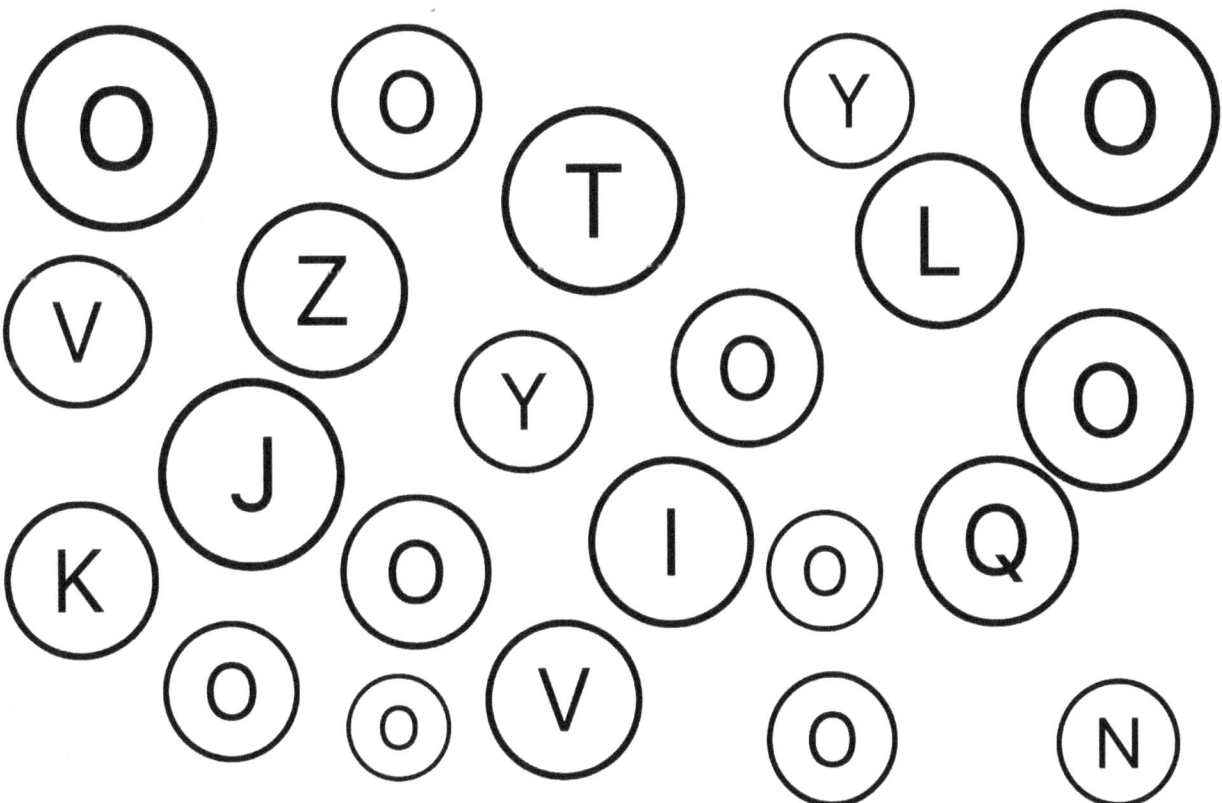

Name: ....

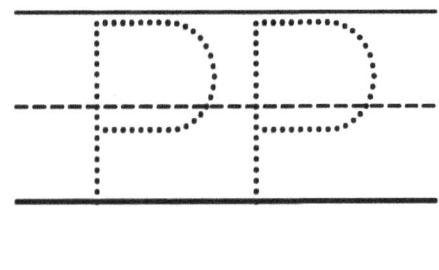

Find the letters

Trace the letters. Then color the circles that have the letter you traced.

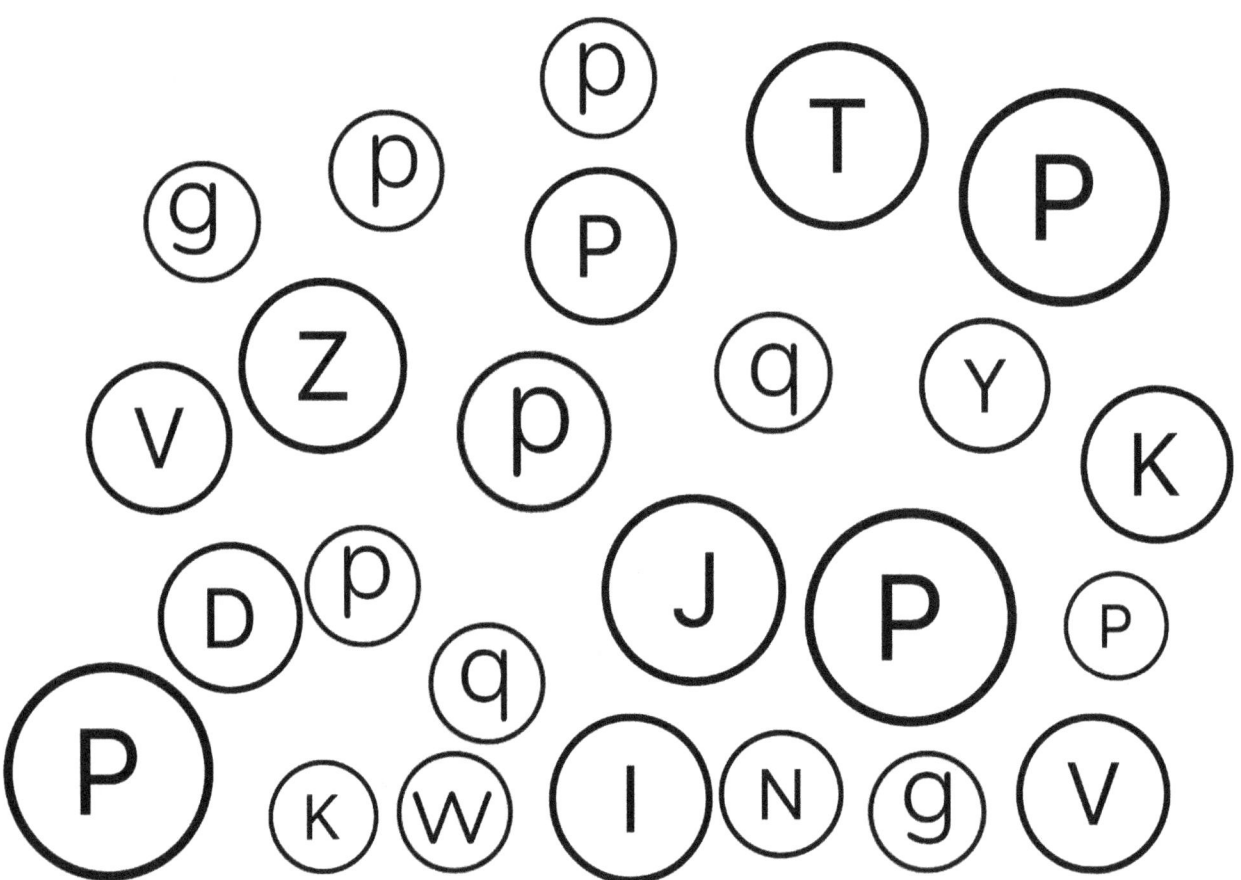

Name: ....

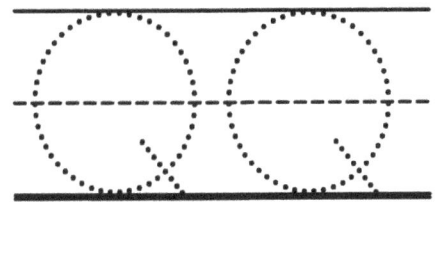

Find the Letters

Trace the letters. Then color the circles that have the letter you traced.

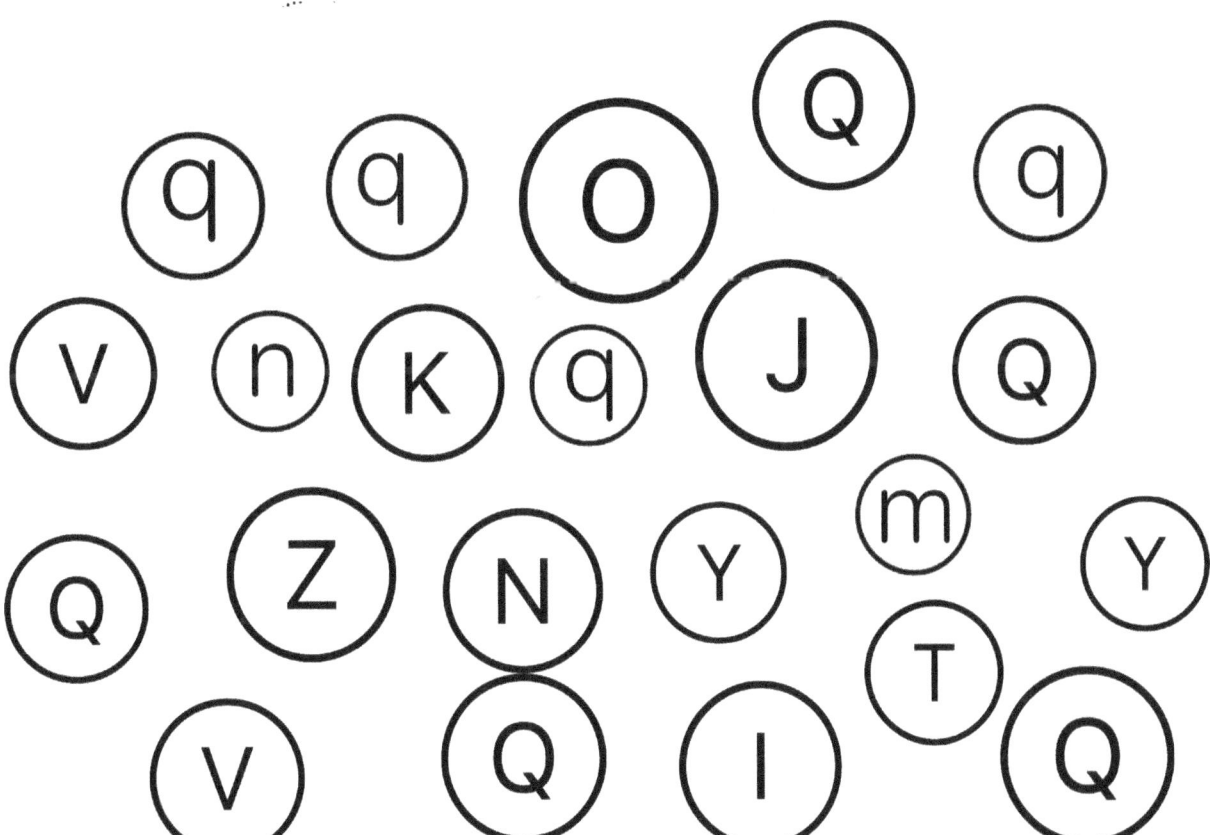

Name: ....

Find the letters

Trace the letters. Then color the circles that have the letter you traced.

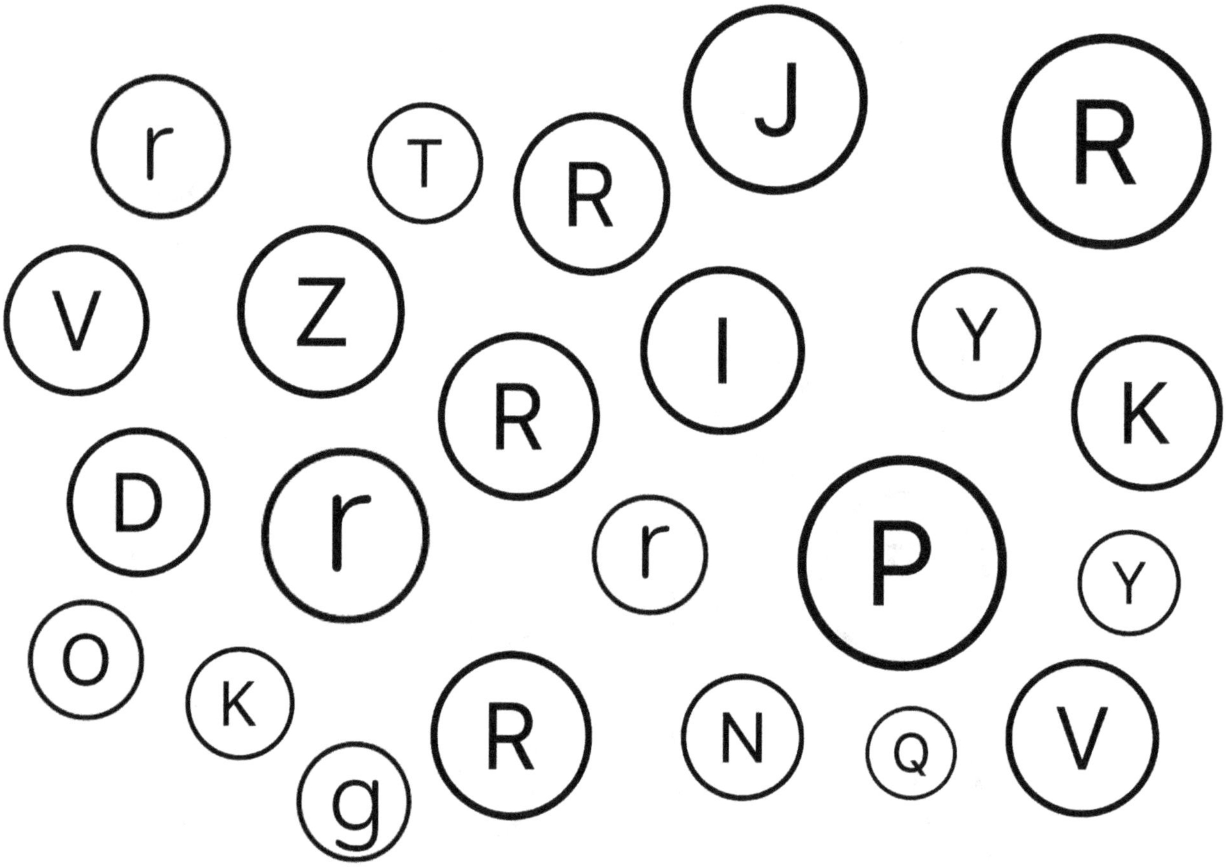

68

Name:

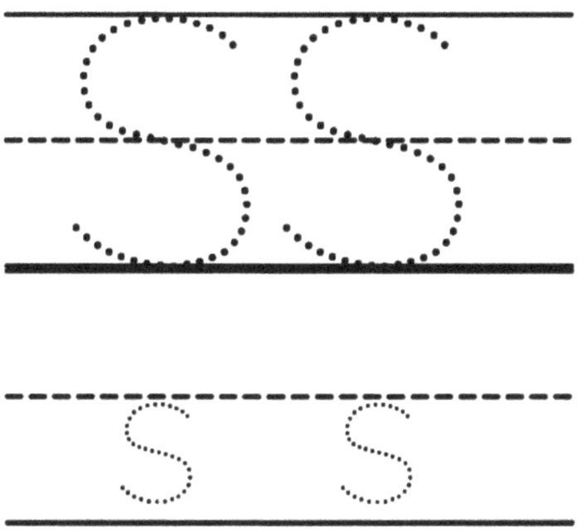

Ss
ss

Find the Letters

Trace the letters. Then color the circles that have the letter you traced.

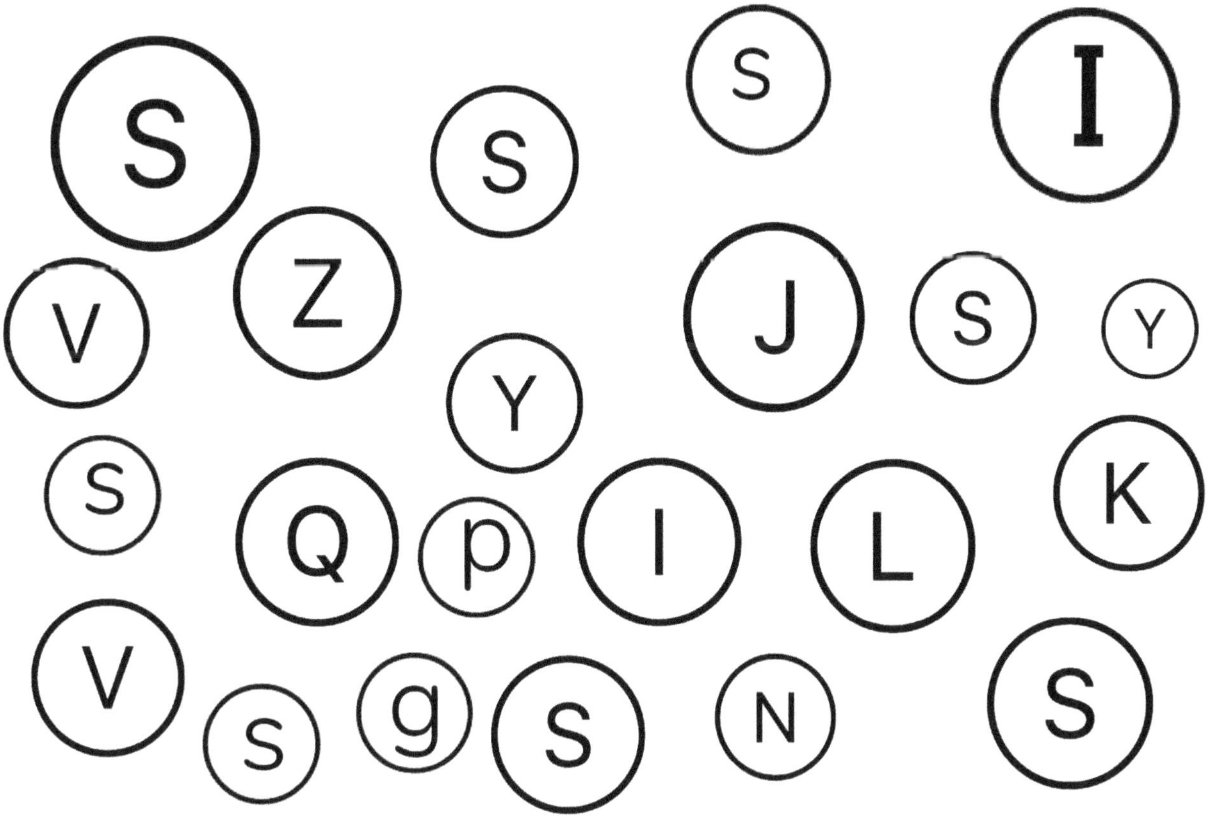

Name:

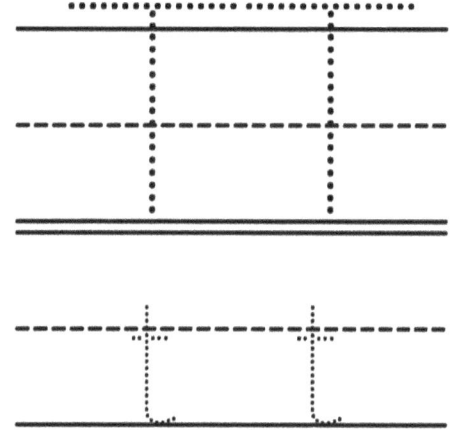

Find the letters

Trace the letters. Then color the circles that have the letter you traced.

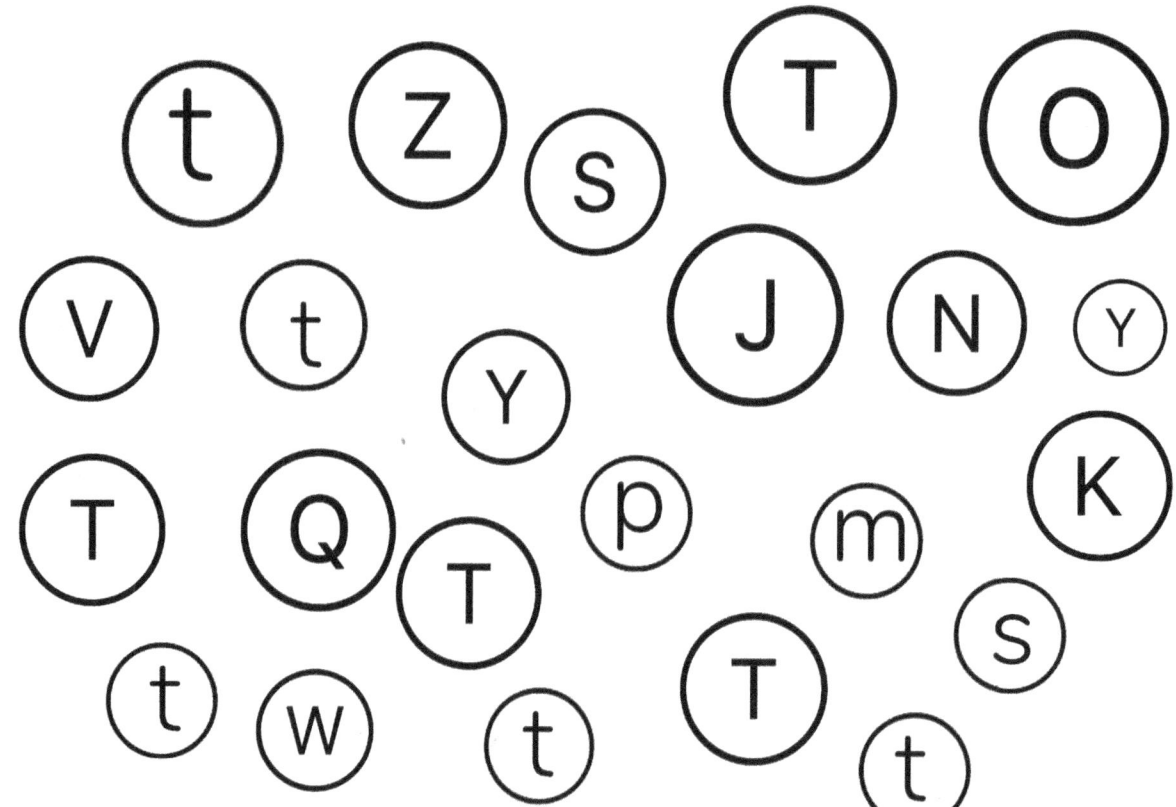

Name: ....

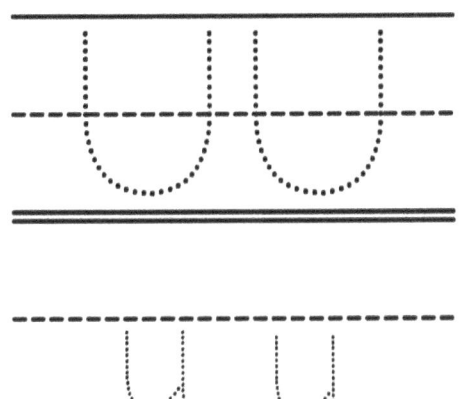

Find the Letters

Trace the letters. Then color the circles that have the letter you traced.

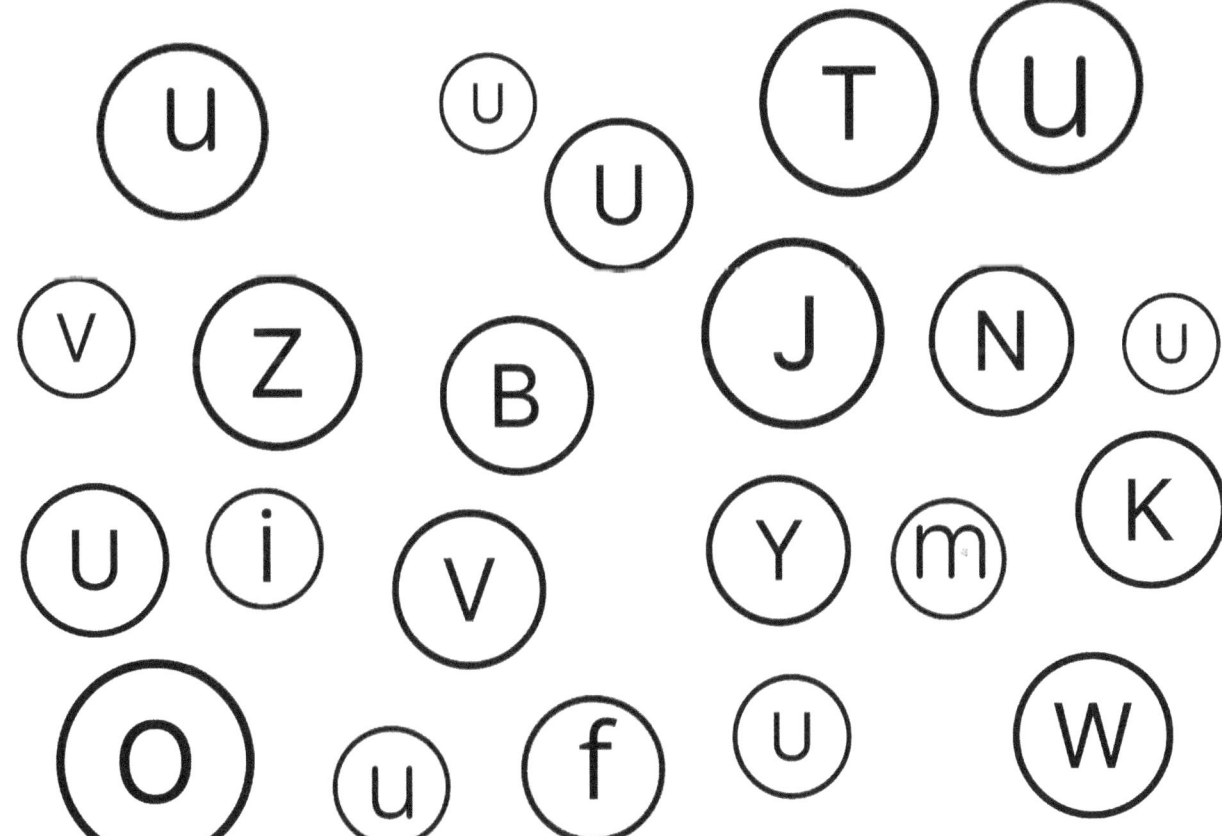

Name:

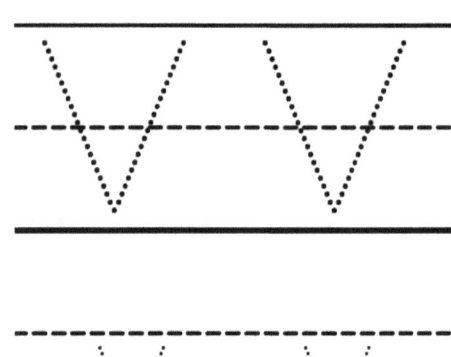

Find the letters

Trace the letters. Then color the circles that have the letter you traced.

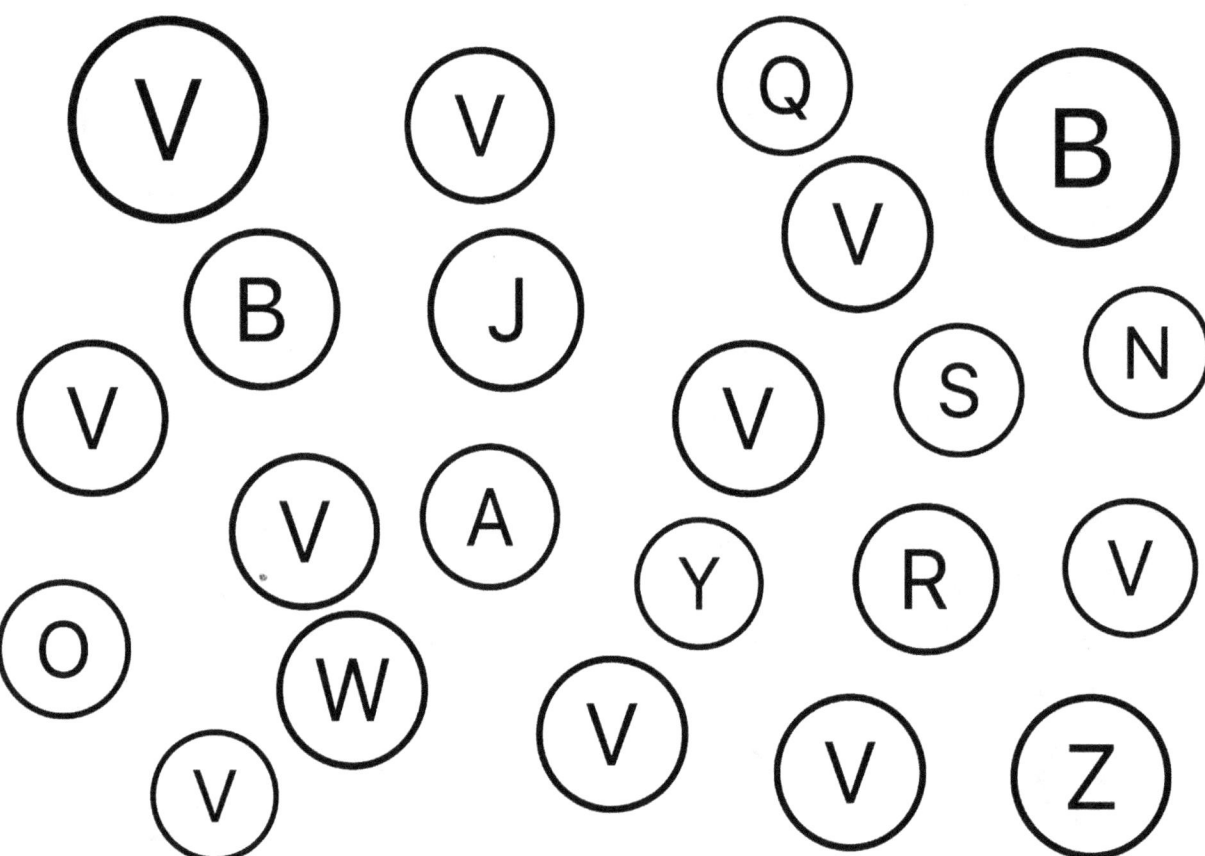

Name: ....

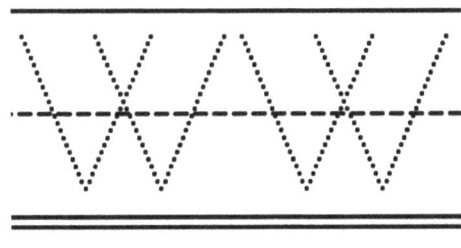

Find the Letters

Trace the letters. Then color the circles that have the letter you traced.

Name: _____

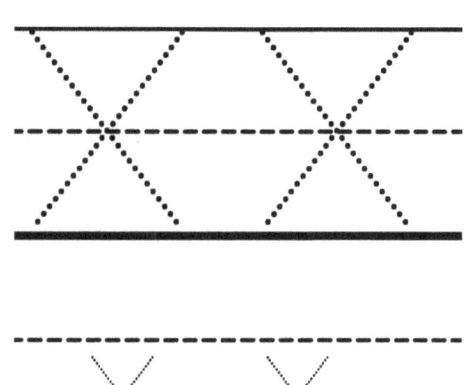

Find the letters

Trace the letters. Then color the circles that have the letter you traced.

Name:

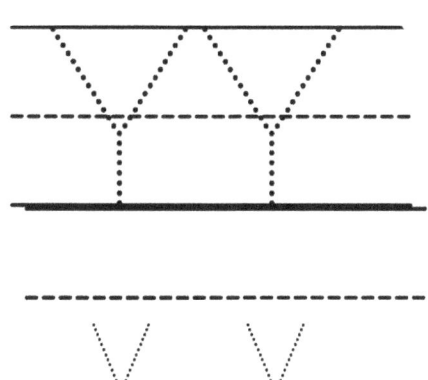

Find the Letters

Trace the letters. Then color the circles that have the letter you traced.

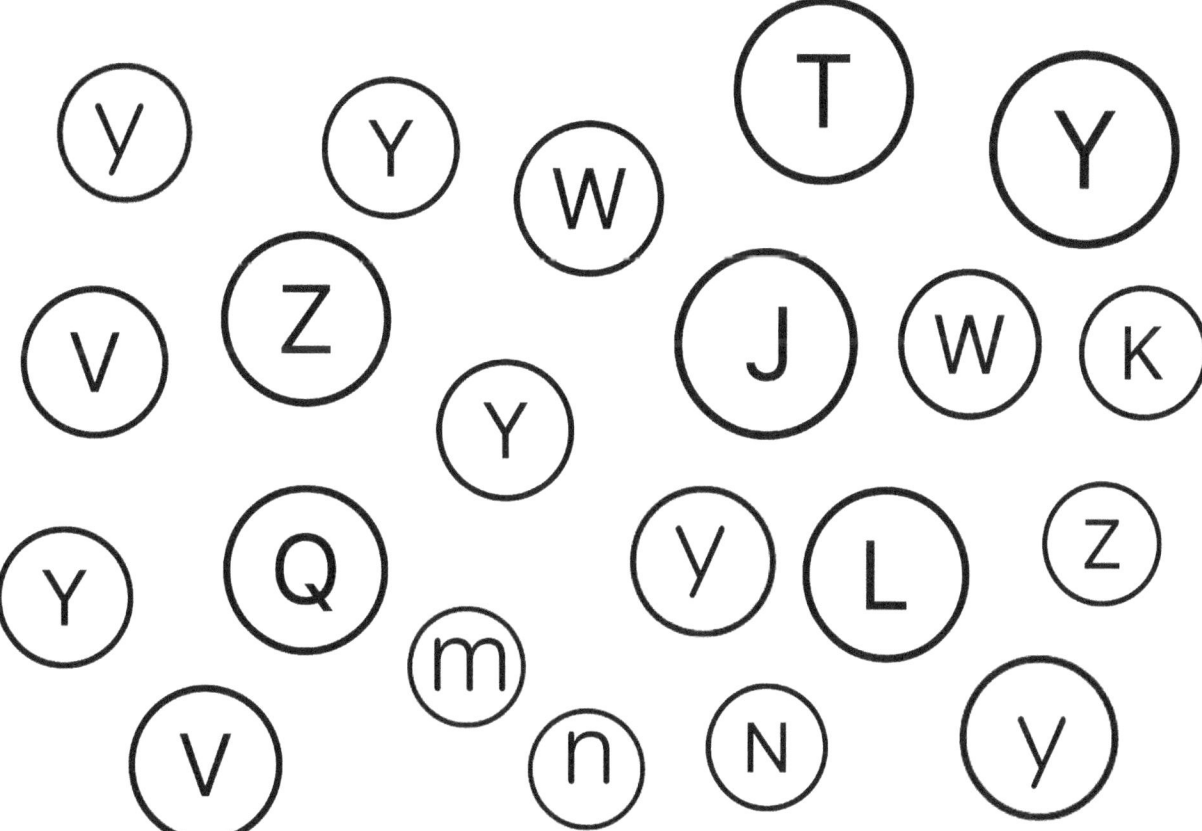

Name: _____

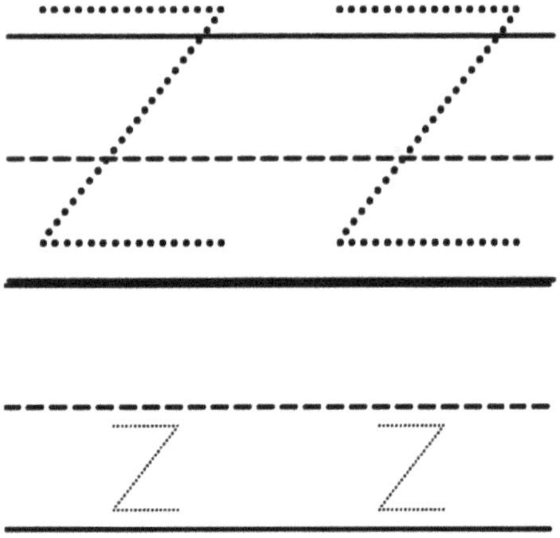

Z Z
Z Z
Z Z

Find the letters

Trace the letters. Then color the circles that have the letter you traced.

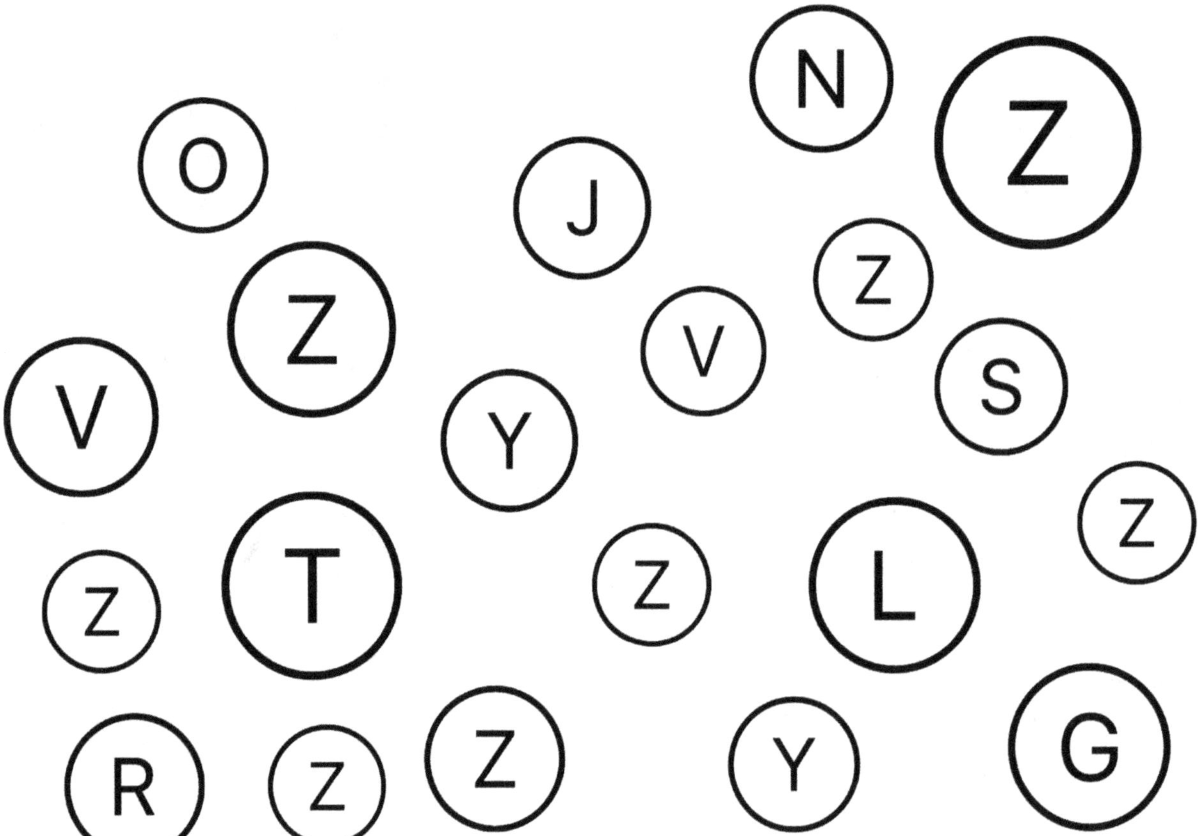

Name:

Trace the letters. Then write the letters at the bottom.

A B C D E F G
H I J K L M N
O P Q R S T
U V W X Y Z

Connect the dots from A — Z

Connect the dots from A — Z

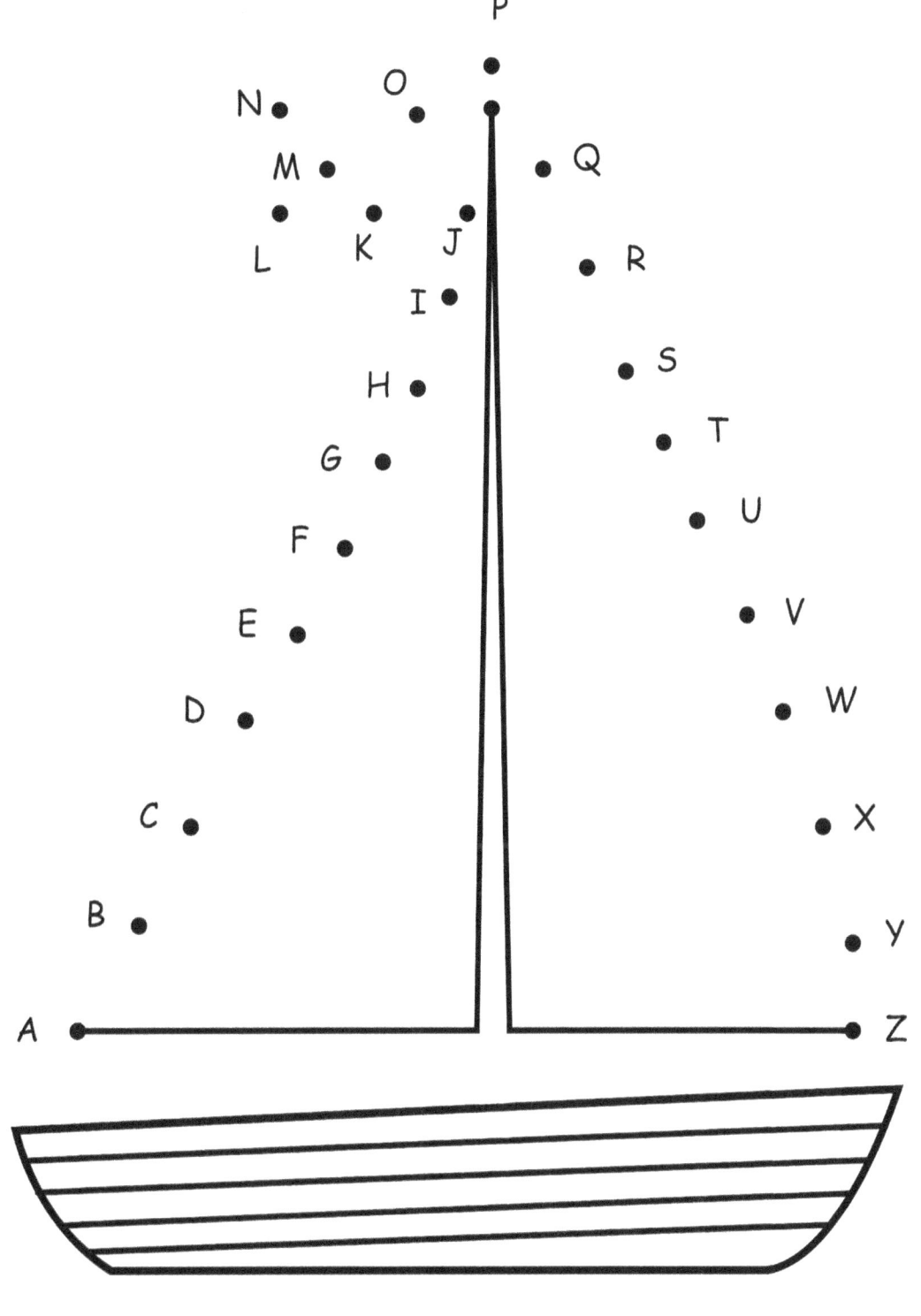

Connect the dots from A — Z

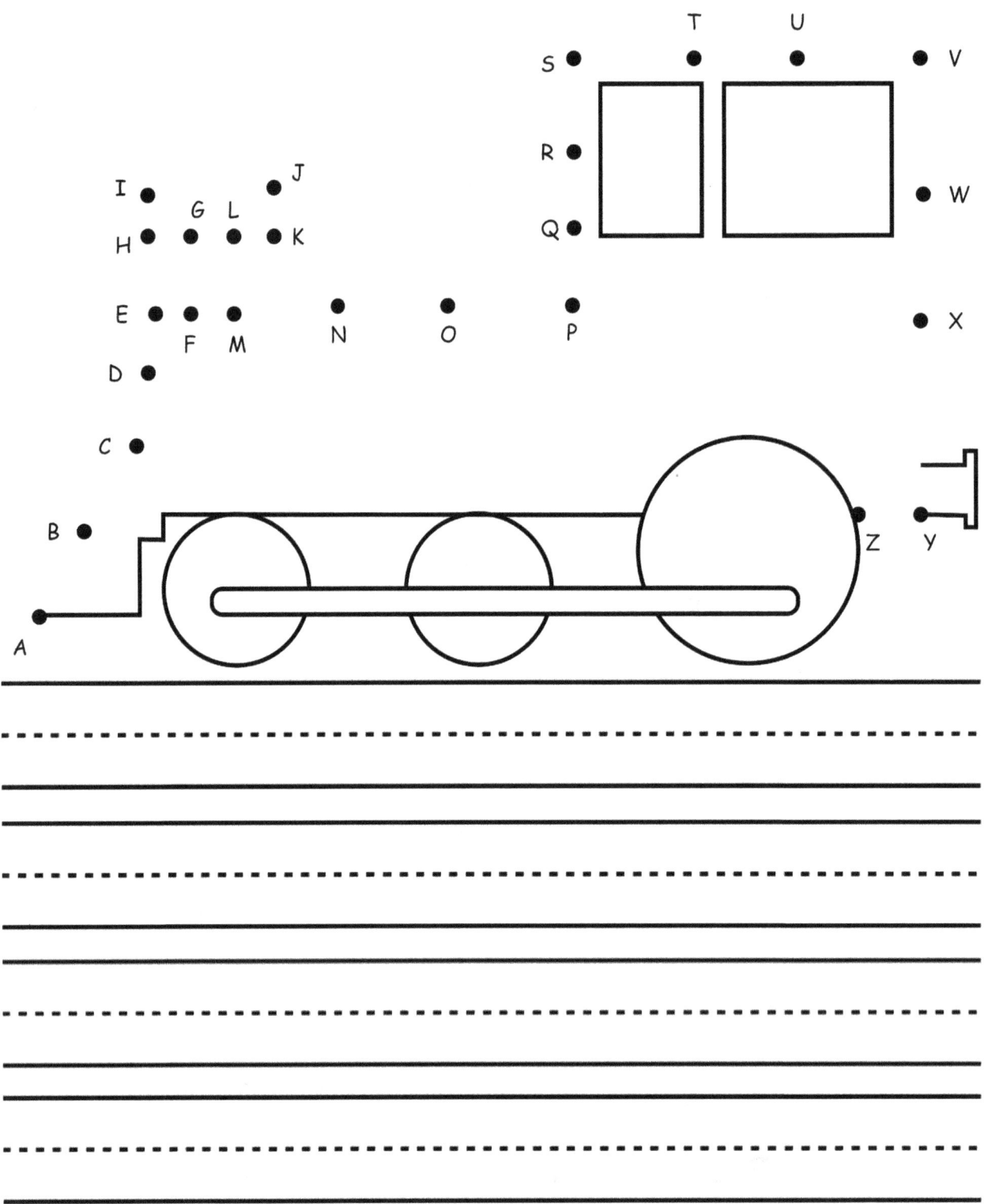

Connect the dots from A — Z

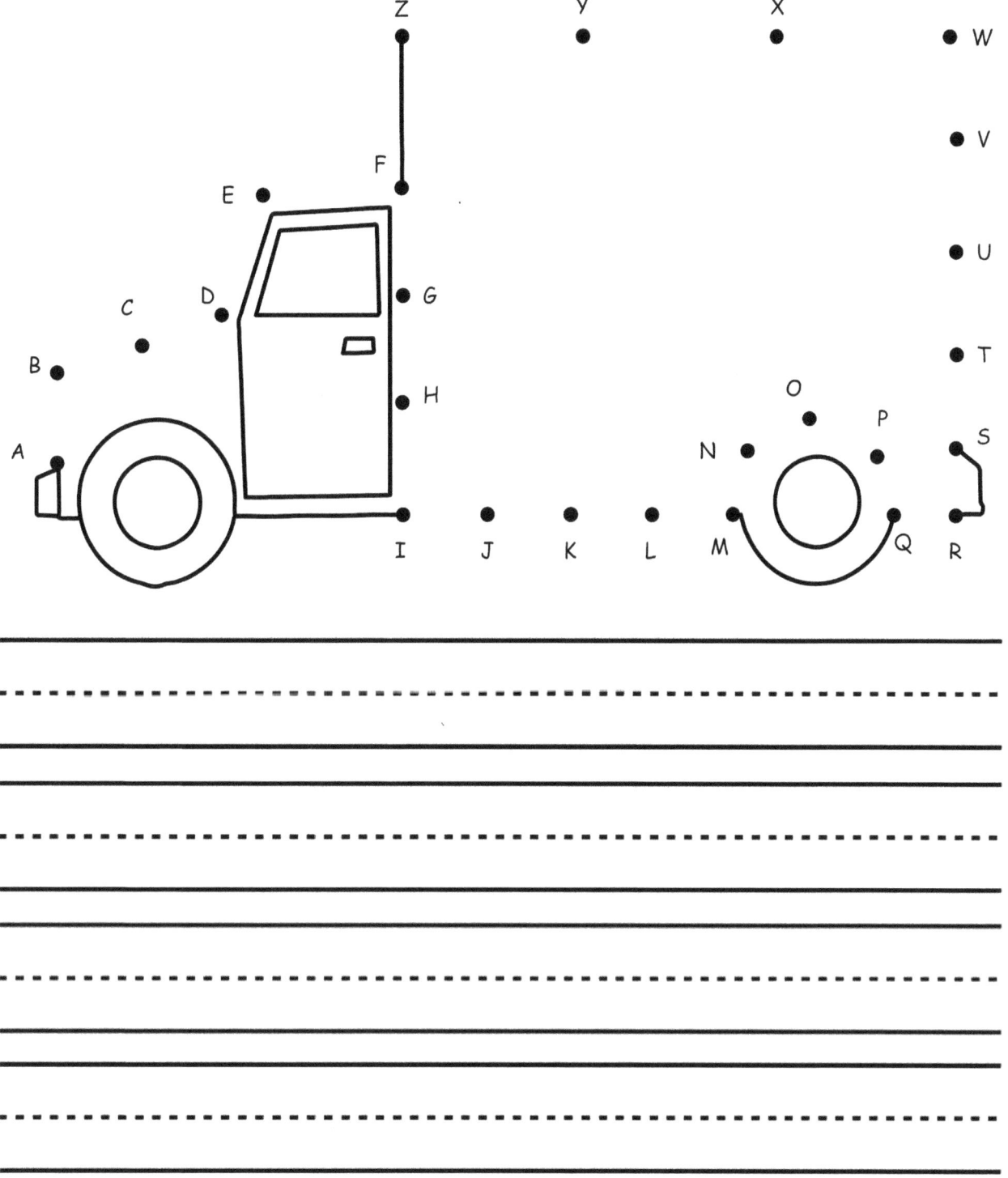

Connect the dots from A — Z

More Alphabet Pratice

Circle all the uppercase letters and lowercase letters you find. Write how many you counted.

Circle all the A's and a's.

B	I	o	A	A	a	o	p	n	m	o	a	e	r	g	y	a	z	c
G	y	a	a	d	q	p	A	B	P	X	Z	A	e	A	U	F	C	A

How many uppercase A's did you find? ☐   How many lowercase a's did you find? ☐

Circle all the B's and b's.

B	I	o	B	A	a	o	b	n	m	o	a	e	r	g	y	b	b	c
G	b	a	b	d	q	p	A	B	P	B	Z	A	e	A	U	F	C	b

How many uppercase B's did you find? ☐   How many lowercase b's did you find? ☐

Circle all the C's and c's.

S	I	o	C	A	a	c	b	n	m	C	a	c	r	g	y	C	b	c
G	c	a	b	C	q	p	A	B	P	C	Z	c	e	A	U	F	C	b

How many uppercase C's did you find? ☐   How many lowercase c's did you find? ☐

Circle all the D's and d's.

D	I	x	C	A	a	d	b	n	D	C	a	d	g	y	D	b	c	y
D	c	m	D	q	d	A	B	P	C	Z	w	d	A	D	F	C	b	s

How many uppercase D's did you find? ☐   How many lowercase d's did you find? ☐

More Alphabet Pratice

Circle all the uppercase letters and lowercase letters you find. Write how many you counted.

Circle all the E's and e's.

E	v	o	C	E	a	d	b	w	D	E	a	d	e	u	D	e	c	c
D	c	e	D	q	S	E	B	e	C	Z	c	d	A	E	F	C	e	x

How many uppercase E's did you find? ☐   How many lowercase e's did you find? ☐

Circle all the F's and f's.

f	I	F	C	E	a	d	f	w	D	E	a	f	f	F	D	e	F	j
D	f	S	F	f	p	E	F	e	F	Z	c	d	O	E	F	f	e	y

How many uppercase F's did you find? ☐   How many lowercase f's did you find? ☐

Circle all the G's and g's.

G	g	I	S	C	G	a	d	g	G	D	G	a	f	g	H	D	e	F
X	f	G	g	M	g	G	F	e	F	Z	c	d	A	E	G	f	e	G

How many uppercase G's did you find? ☐   How many lowercase g's did you find? ☐

Circle all the H's and h's.

s	h	X	C	E	H	d	h	n	D	E	a	H	f	h	D	H	F	h
D	h	e	F	H	p	E	h	e	F	H	c	d	H	E	F	h	h	b

How many uppercase H's did you find? ☐   How many lowercase h's did you find? ☐

More Alphabet Pratice

Circle all the uppercase letters and lowercase letters you find. Write how many you counted.

Circle all the I's and i's.

S	I	i	I	E	a	d	f	n	D	E	a	I	f	F	D	I	F	D
D	H	e	F	I	p	E	F	e	i	Z	c	d	A	E	F	f	I	H

How many uppercase I's did you find? ☐   How many lowercase i's did you find? ☐

Circle all the J's and j's.

s	J	j	F	C	j	a	m	f	n	J	E	a	J	f	J	D	j	F
D	f	e	F	f	j	n	F	e	F	Z	c	d	A	s	J	f	e	o

How many uppercase J's did you find? ☐   How many lowercase j's did you find? ☐

Circle all the K's and k's.

f	k	H	C	K	a	d	f	n	k	E	S	f	f	F	K	k	F
D	k	K	F	Z	K	E	F	K	k	Z	K	d	A	E	K	f	e

How many uppercase K's did you find? ☐   How many lowercase k's did you find? ☐

Circle all the L's and l's.

S	I	g	L	E	a	L	f	n	D	E	l	o	f	F	L	I	L	k
D	f	l	w	L	p	l	F	e	F	L	R	d	A	E	b	l	e	s

How many uppercase L's did you find? ☐   How many lowercase l's did you find? ☐

More Alphabet Pratice

Circle all the uppercase letters and lowercase letters you find. Write how many you counted.

Circle all the M's and m's.

f	M	s	B	z	m	d	m	n	m	E	m	f	j	M	D	e	F	u
D	m	e	M	f	o	t	M	e	F	Z	s	d	A	M	F	f	e	p

How many uppercase M's did you find? ☐   How many lowercase m's did you find? ☐

Circle all the N's and n's.

R	N	F	N	N	a	n	f	w	D	E	a	f	f	F	D	e	N
D	s	x	F	f	s	n	F	e	F	n	k	d	A	E	F	f	e

How many uppercase N's did you find? ☐   How many lowercase n's did you find? ☐

Circle all the O's and o's.

R	I	o	C	E	O	d	f	n	O	o	o	f	f	F	O	o	F	x
D	O	e	F	f	o	S	O	e	F	Z	c	d	A	K	o	f	e	w

How many uppercase O's did you find? ☐   How many lowercase o's did you find? ☐

Circle all the P's and p's.

P	I	p	C	P	a	p	f	P	D	P	a	P	P	F	P	e	F	p
G	P	p	F	f	p	P	F	P	F	Z	P	d	A	P	F	f	e	p

How many uppercase P's did you find? ☐   How many lowercase p's did you find? ☐

More Alphabet Pratice

Circle all the uppercase letters and lowercase letters you find. Write how many you counted.

Circle all the Q's and q's.

q	u	s	H	E	a	d	f	Q	D	E	a	f	Q	F	D	e	I	v
D	f	Q	q	Y	p	E	F	q	F	Z	c	Q	Q	E	F	f	e	Q

How many uppercase Q's did you find? ☐ How many lowercase q's did you find? ☐

Circle all the R's and r's.

d	R	v	r	E	a	r	f	R	D	Z	a	R	F	F	R	e	F	b
D	L	e	Y	R	p	E	r	e	F	Z	c	d	A	E	F	f	e	R

How many uppercase R's did you find? ☐ How many lowercase r's did you find? ☐

Circle all the S's and s's.

S	I	s	C	E	a	d	f	S	D	E	a	S	b	s	S	e	F	n
S	S	e	T	x	w	E	w	e	S	Z	s	o	A	E	F	f	e	s

How many uppercase S's did you find? ☐ How many lowercase s's did you find? ☐

Circle all the T's and t's.

w	I	Q	T	t	T	T	T	n	D	E	a	t	s	F	D	e	T	t
D	f	t	F	f	t	E	t	e	T	Z	c	T	A	E	G	f	e	p

How many uppercase T's did you find? ☐ How many lowercase t's did you find? ☐

More Alphabet Pratice

Circle all the uppercase letters and lowercase letters you find. Write how many you counted.

Circle all the U's and u's.

m	I	U	C	U	a	d	u	n	D	E	a	u	x	F	U	e	F	k
D	U	z	s	f	u	E	u	e	M	Z	c	d	u	R	F	f	e	w

How many uppercase U's did you find? ☐   How many lowercase u's did you find? ☐

Circle all the V's and v's.

f	I	V	V	S	a	d	S	n	D	E	N	v	f	F	v	e	F	s
v	f	v	F	f	p	V	F	e	F	V	O	v	A	V	F	f	e	j

How many uppercase V's did you find? ☐   How many lowercase v's did you find? ☐

Circle all the W's and w's.

A	I	W	C	W	x	d	w	n	D	w	a	o	W	w	D	e	F	b
t	w	e	w	f	p	s	F	e	W	Z	W	d	A	E	F	f	e	W

How many uppercase W's did you find? ☐   How many lowercase w's did you find? ☐

Circle all the X's and x's.

h	I	X	H	E	a	x	x	n	D	E	a	f	f	F	D	f	F	s
D	x	e	F	f	p	X	F	e	F	Z	X	s	A	E	X	f	e	X

How many uppercase X's did you find? ☐   How many lowercase x's did you find? ☐

More Alphabet Pratice

Circle all the uppercase letters and lowercase letters you find. Write how many you counted.

Circle all the Y's and y's.

Y	I	d	C	y	M	Y	f	n	D	y	a	f	f	K	D	e	F	y
D	f	e	y	Y	p	E	F	e	F	Z	Y	d	y	Y	F	f	e	p

How many uppercase Y's did you find? ☐   How many lowercase y's did you find? ☐

Circle all the Z's and z's.

Z	I	F	Z	E	m	d	Z	n	D	E	Z	S	A	Z	D	e	F	m
D	z	e	Z	z	p	Z	F	e	F	Z	c	d	A	E	F	f	z	c

How many uppercase Z's did you find? ☐   How many lowercase z's did you find? ☐

My Brain is Strong! I Did It!

Color your brain your favorite color.

**Look at the pictures.
Write your spelling words.**

Look at the picture.
Write your spelling words.

91

Look at the picture.
Write your spelling words.

Look at the picture.
Write your spelling words.

Look at the picture.
Write your spelling words.

Write your favorite spelling words.

PHONICS and READING

What is Taught, When it is Taught, Who is Being Taught, and Who is Teaching, are critically important for early learners. With a strong emphasis on learning to read "phonetically," we believe children can gain the confidence to learn using the most updated educational materials while in a secure environment. Liberia Literary Society strives to work together with teachers to mentor them as they work to educate children. We are passionate about working for children and making this world a better one for them, and helping them succeed in the classroom and beyond.

The aim and objective of Teacher Jeanette GETTING STARTED WITH ABC AND 123 workbook is to prepare students for their educational journey with a solid start. Starting with the alphabet, let's begin with teaching phonics to help children learn the alphabetical principle, the idea that letters represent the sounds of spoken language and that there is an organized, consistent, and predictable relationship between written letters and spoken sounds.

Let's first understand what phonics is. Phonics is a way of teaching children how to read and write. It helps them hear, identify, and use different sounds that distinguish one word from another in the English language. Phonics involves matching the sounds of spoken English with individual letters or groups of letters. For example, the sound k can be spelled as c, k, ck or ch. Teaching children to blend the sounds of letters together helps them decode unfamiliar or unknown words by sounding them out. Help your students understand the sounds of alphabets.

PHONICS and READING

Phonics is matching the sounds of spoken English with individual letters or groups of letters. It is used to teach children the relationship between letters and the sounds that they make. Phonics is all about using sounds to read words.

Tap and blend

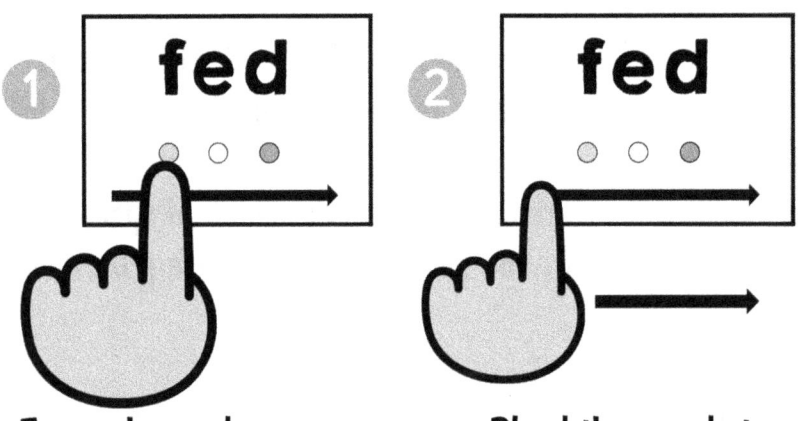

Tap each sound   Blend the sounds to read the word.

1. Using their workbook, first, let students tap out each individual sound in the word.
2. Then, students should blend the sounds to read the word smoothly. This is done as the student moves his or her finger on the arrow from left to right.
3. To help students build fluency, have students practice tapping the words a few times then ask them to blend the sounds without tapping first.

Beginning Sounds. What do you hear?
Say the name of each picture.

1. Remind students the sound of the focus letter. For example, the letter A sounds like /a/.
2. Ask students why it is important to know the beginning sounds of words. Possible answers could be that it helps with reading, and it helps with writing. Explain these answers.
3. Show students the sorting pictures in their workbook on page 96-100.
4. Allow students to follow the <u>Tap and Blend</u> to complete the Beginning Sounds of each of the alphabet A - Z.

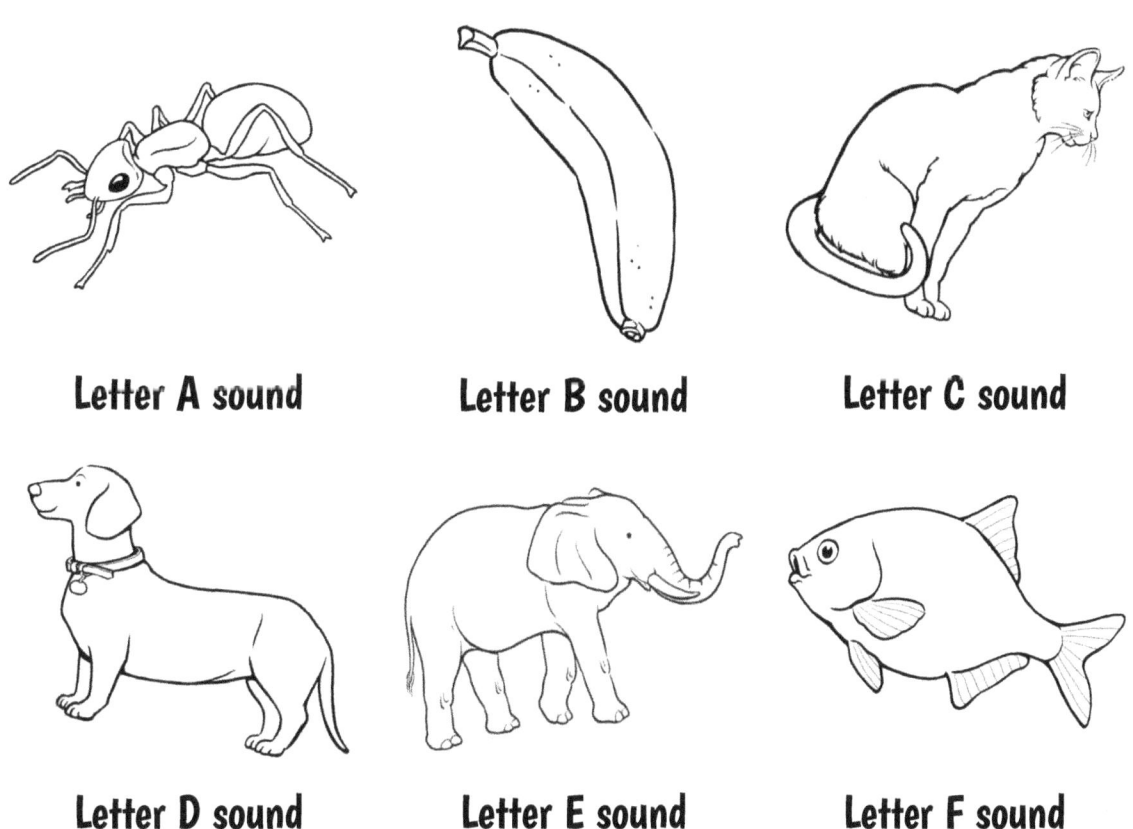

Letter A sound   Letter B sound   Letter C sound

Letter D sound   Letter E sound   Letter F sound

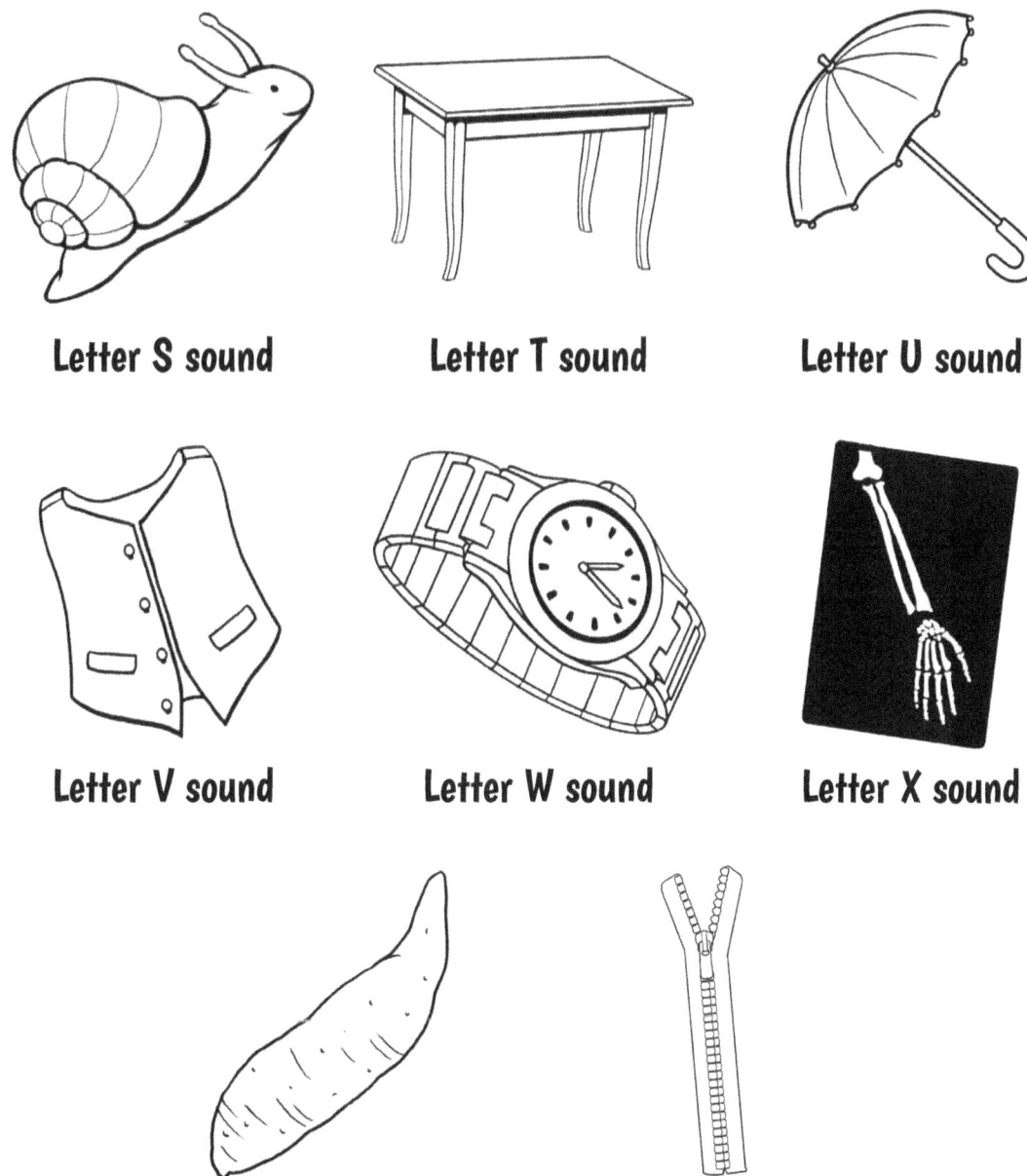

Letter S sound

Letter T sound

Letter U sound

Letter V sound

Letter W sound

Letter X sound

Letter Y sound

Letter Z sound

Phonics Sounds Worksheets

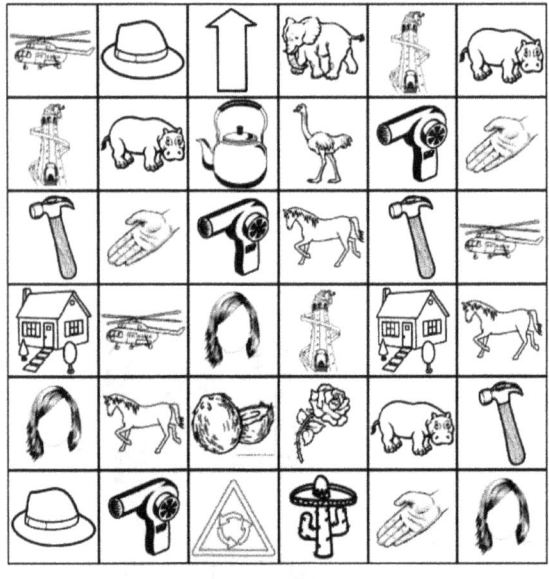

Color the square with pictures that begin with the /h/ sound to find the hidden letter.

Trace uppercase M.
Color the pictures that begin with the /m/ sound.

Color the pictures that begin with the /t/ sound.
What is the hidden letter?

Write the letter of the beginning sounds.

Let's teach the sounds of the alphabet!

A   say /a/ as you can hear this in apple, ant, alligator.

B   say the sound /b/ as you can hear this in bat, balloon, baby.

C   say /c/ as in Car, Cap, Cub.

D   say /d/ as in Drum, Dog, Doll

E   try to break an imaginary egg in your hand and say /e/ As in Egg, Eggplant

F   say /f/ as in Fish, Frog

G   say /g/ as in Grapes, Gate

H   say /h/ as in Horse, Hat, Hen

I   say /i/ as in Inkpot, Igloo

J   say /j/ as in Jam, Jar

K   say /k/ as in Kettle, Kite

L   Put your finger in front of your mouth and roll your tongue behind your teeth and say /l/

M   say /m/ as in Mango, Moon

N   say /n/ as in Nose, Net

Let's teach the sounds of the alphabet!

O say /o/ as in Orange, Octopus

P Hold one finger in front of your mouth as it is a candle and blow slowly and say /p/ as in Pig, Pan

Q say /qu/ as in Quack, Quilt, Queen

R say /r/ as in Rat, Rabbit, Rain

S say /s/ as in Socks, Six, Snail

T say /t/ as in Tree, Tap, Top

U say /u/ as in Up, Umbrella

V Bite your lower lips and say /v/ and feel the vibration on your lips as in vet, van

W Make a O with your lips like a kiss and blow it in your palm and say /w/ as in Watch, Web, Well

X Take an imaginary camera and click and say /ks/ as in Fox, Wax, Box

Y say /y/ as in Yak, Yawn, Yellow

Z say /zzz/ as in Zebra, Zero, Zigzag

Missing Vowels

Look at the pictures and fill in the missing vowel to complete each word.

  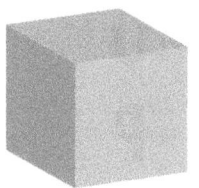

m _ g   c _ t   b _ x

| o | a | u |

r _ g   t _ n   v _ n

| e | a | u |

Missing Vowels
Look at the pictures and fill in the missing vowel to complete each word.

k_t	f_n	b_g
i	u	a

v_n	l_g	h_n
e	o	a

Phonics Sounds Chart

a — cat	e — hen	i — pig	o — fox	u — sun
th — thumb	ch — chicken	sh — shell	wh — whistle	qu — queen
ar — star	or — horse	er — flower	ir — bird	ur — purse
ay — hay	ai — snail	ee — bee	ea — leaf	ea — thread
oa — boat	ow — bowl	ow — cow	ou — cloud	oo — igloo

Sounds Phonics

Sh-	Th-	Ch-	-unk
shark	the	chin	skunk
sheep	that	chomp	bunk
shop	they	chop	dunk
shut	this	chug	junk
she	thumb	chain	sunk
shoe	three	cheer	shrunk
ship	there	chief	stunk
shot	think	check	trunk
shell	thorn	chick	chipmunk

-ink	-ing	-ay	-ai
link	king	bay	snail
pink	sing	day	sail
sink	ring	may	nail
wink	wing	ray	pail
blink	ding	say	tail
drink	spring	way	paint
stink	sting	gray	braid
ink	swing	play	rain
think	string	tray	train

Sounds Phonics

-ee	-ea	-oa	bossy E
bee	beak	road	whale
deer	read	toad	white
feet	peach	foal	snake
see	flea	roar	five
tree	squeak	boat	kite
queen	mean	coat	cone
green	beast	goat	cube
sheep	eat	goal	June
tweet	treat	soap	name

vowel walk	oo (as in boot)
blue	moo
glue	food
fruit	zoo
suit	roof
die	pool
pie	school
tie	broom
clue	spoon
cried	goose

Learning Objectives
Students will be able to identify letters and letter sounds at the beginning and end of words.

a	e	i	o	u
cat	hen	pig	fox	sun

bag	Ben	big	Bob	bug
bat	egg	did	dog	fun
dad	fed	fib	fog	gum
fan	hen	him	got	Gus
jam	leg	Jill	hot	hug
mat	men	lid	job	mud
nap	pet	pig	log	pup
pan	red	rib	not	rug
wag	ten	sip	mop	sun
Sam	wet	win	top	tub

Learning Objectives
Students will be able to identify letters and letter sounds at the beginning and end of words.

Let's move on to CVC words.

A CVC word is a single syllable three phoneme sound word that follows the pattern of a consonant sound, vowel sound, consonant sound. Students should learn to speak out the word by blending it letter by letter.

Discuss CVC segment and blend.

Teach the students to speak out the word by blending it letter by letter. What is blending and segmenting?

Blending is the process of combining sounds together to create a word.

Segmenting is the process of breaking a word down into its individual sounds.

Blending links to reading, segmenting to writing. Therefore, blending should always come before segmenting. For example, the word cat is made up of three sounds — C / A / T — Together these sounds produce the spoken word cat. Whereas in segmenting, the word cat is made up of three phonemes — beginning, middle and end.

Learning Objectives
Students will be able to identify letters and letter sounds at the beginning and end of words.

	\multicolumn{9}{c}{Use this list of CVC words to plan a lesson or use it as a reference.}
A	bad	bag	bat	can	cap	cat	dab	dad	fan
	fat	gal	gap	gas	hat	jab	jam	lab	lap
	mad	man	mat	nag	nap	pal	pan	pat	rag
	ram	rat	sap	sat	tan	tap	van	wag	zap
E	bed	beg	bet	den	fed	gel	get	hen	hex
	jet	led	leg	let	men	met	net	peg	pen
	pet	red	ref	set	ten	vet	web	wet	ze
I	bid	big	bin	bit	did	dig	din	dip	fib
	fig	fin	fit	fix	gig	hid	him	hip	his
	hit	jig	kid	kit	lid	lip	lit	nip	mit
	mix	pig	pin	pit	rid	rig	rim	rip	sin
	sip	sit	six	tin	tip	wig	win	wit	zip
O	bob	bog	box	cop	cot	dog	dot	fog	fox
	gob	got	hog	hop	hot	job	jog	jot	lob
	log	lot	mom	mob	nod	not	pop	pot	rob
	rod	rot	sob	sod	son	ton	top	tot	won
U	bud	bug	bum	bun	bus	but	cub	cup	cut
	dug	fun	gum	gun	gut	hug	hum	hut	lug
	jug	jut	mud	mug	nun	nut	pug	put	pun
	rub	rug	run	rut	sub	sum	sun	tub	tug

Let's understand a new concept, blends and digraphs.

A blend contains two consonants, each making one sound, such as S and L. Two different consonants, but one, they are together;

they make one sound, sl. Think about the word slide; you can clearly hear the sound of S and L separately. Here, they both keep their sounds.

A digraph contains two letters that combine together to correspond to make one sound such as SH, V, CH, TH. Think about the word sheep, you can hear that SH makes one sound.

Tap each sound   Blend the sounds to read the word.

1. Using their workbook, first, let students tap out each individual sound in the word.
2. Then, students should blend the sounds to read the word smoothly. This is done as the student moves his or her finger on the arrow from left to right.
3. To help students build fluency, have students practice tapping the words a few times then ask them to blend the sounds without tapping first.

My Blends Chart

bl	cl	fl	gl	pl
blue	clown	fly	glove	plane |//
sl	**br**	**cr**	**dr**	**fr**
slide	branch	crab	drum	frog
gr	**pr**	**tr**	**wr**	**thr**
grapes	prize	tree	write	throw
st	**sp**	**sn**	**sc**	**sk**
star	spider	snail	scared	skate
sm	**sw**	**tw**		
smile	swing	twins		

Beginning Blends

l blends

cl
fl
gl
pl
sl

clown
flower
glue
plane
slide

r blends

br
cr
dr
fr
gr
tr

brush
crayon
drum
frog
grape
tree

s blends

sk
sl
sm
sn
sp
st

skate
smile
snail
spider
stamp

Beginning Blends

h digraphs

cheese
phone
shoe
thumb
wheel

Learning Objectives
Students will be able to identify letters and letter sounds at the beginning and end of words.

Ending Blends and Digraphs

A digraph is a blend of two letters that makes a sound.

gift
hand
tent

first
desk
swing

Kindergarten Sight Word List

Let's now discuss sight words.

Sight words are the words that appear most frequently in our reading and writing, as these are common words that a child recognizes instantly without sounding them. Many sight words are tricky to read and spell as they aren't spelled the way they sound. Therefore, sight words are often very tricky for students to sound out. Recognizing words by sight helps children become fast readers. According to a study, up to 75% of the words used in text written for young readers are sight words.

For example: I, you, he, she, with, this, that, come, some, etc.

The goal is for all Kindergarteners to know 100 sight words by the end of the school year. Once students have learned the alphabet, they can start learning their sight words. Teach 10 new words each month. By the end of the school year, when the students learn these 100 sight words they will be ready for kindergarten and able to read simple stories! Please practice these words with your students every week.

Sight Word List

List 1	List 2	List 3	List 4	List 5
I	like	to	are	do
can	a	have	for	and
we	see	is	you	what
the	go	play	this	little
at	in	come	here	his
am	of	on	she	two
it	us	be	run	love
up	by	big	off	but
no	eat	one	so	all
yes	was	has	want	saw

Sight Word List

List 6	List 7	List 8	List 9	List 10
said	he	my	five	yellow
there	as	me	seven	red
him	look	where	eight	blue
that	with	jump	your	white
got	they	went	because	black
not	three	four	out	brown
too	six	ten	from	green
why	where	get	who	purple
first	day	away	her	pink
new	could	came	then	nine

Sight Word Pratice

Say the word:

a

Trace the word:

a

Write the word:

Color the word:

a

Circle the sight word:

a	d	l
a	p	a
b	r	a

Color the letters in the sight word:

a	i	e	d	r
y	s	u	l	n
p	k	h	f	e

Complete the sentence:

I can see _____ frog.

Say the word:
and

Trace the word:
and

Write the word:

Color the word:
and

Circle the sight word:

and	end	and
are	ant	and
and	amd	arm

Color the letters in the sight word:

a	i	e	d	r
y	s	u	l	n
p	k	h	f	e

Complete the sentence:
I like cats____dogs.

120

Say the word: go

Trace the word: go

Write the word:

Color the word: go

Circle the sight word:

go	to	so
ge	go	og
go	no	go

Color the letters in the sight word:

t	i	e	d	g
y	s	o	l	n
p	k	h	f	e

Complete the sentence:

I can ___ for a run.

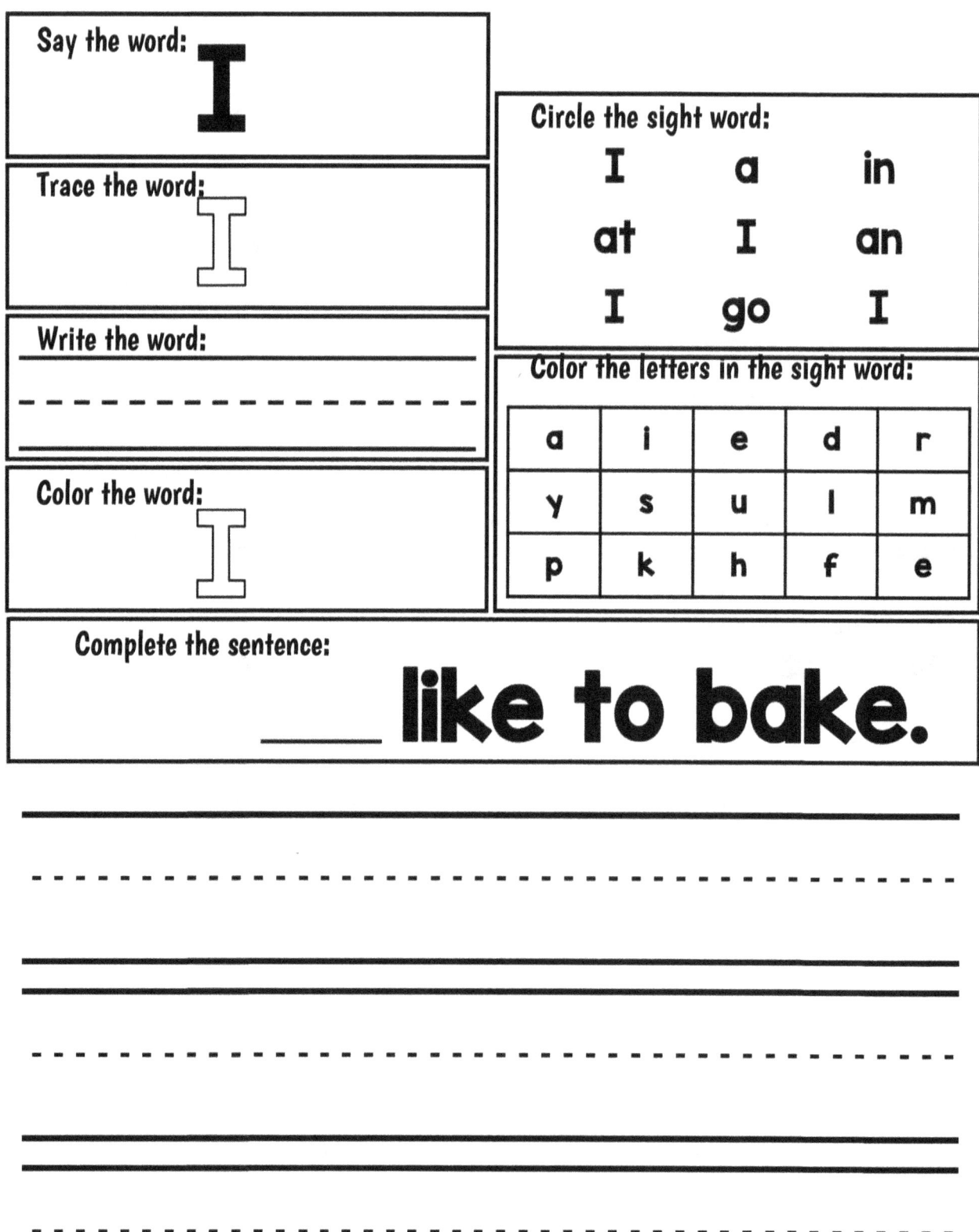

Say the word: **is**

Trace the word: is

Write the word:

Color the word: is

Circle the sight word:

in   is   it
is   if   is
id   is   iz

Color the letters in the sight word:

t	i	e	d	r
y	s	u	l	n
p	k	h	f	e

Complete the sentence:

My hat ___ red.

Say the word: me

Trace the word: me

Write the word: _____

Color the word: me

Circle the sight word:

be	me	my
am	me	he
me	me	mr

Color the letters in the sight word:

o	i	e	m	r
a	k	j	l	n
p	l	o	f	t

Complete the sentence:

She likes _____ .

Say the word:

my

Trace the word:

my

Write the word:

Color the word:

my

Circle the sight word:

me	mo	my
my	ma	my
my	man	me

Color the letters in the sight word:

t	i	e	d	r
y	s	u	l	n
p	k	h	f	m

Complete the sentence:

_____ name is Sam.

Say the word:
see

Trace the word:
see

Write the word:

Color the word:
see

Circle the sight word:

see	bee	sea
see	tee	see
she	see	sew

Color the letters in the sight word:

a	i	e	d	r
y	s	u	l	m
p	k	h	f	e

Complete the sentence:

I _____ a cat.

Say the word: **the**

Trace the word: the

Write the word:

Color the word: the

Circle the sight word:

ten	tee	the
that	the	this
the	tie	the

Color the letters in the sight word:

t	i	e	d	r
y	s	u	l	n
p	k	h	f	e

Complete the sentence:

_____ **cat is black.**

Say the word: to

Trace the word: to

Write the word:

Color the word: to

Circle the sight word:

no	to	it
to	so	to
on	to	too

Color the letters in the sight word:

t	i	e	d	r
y	s	u	l	n
p	k	h	f	o

Complete the sentence:

Let's walk ___ school.

Numbers

My Brain is Ready to Grow!

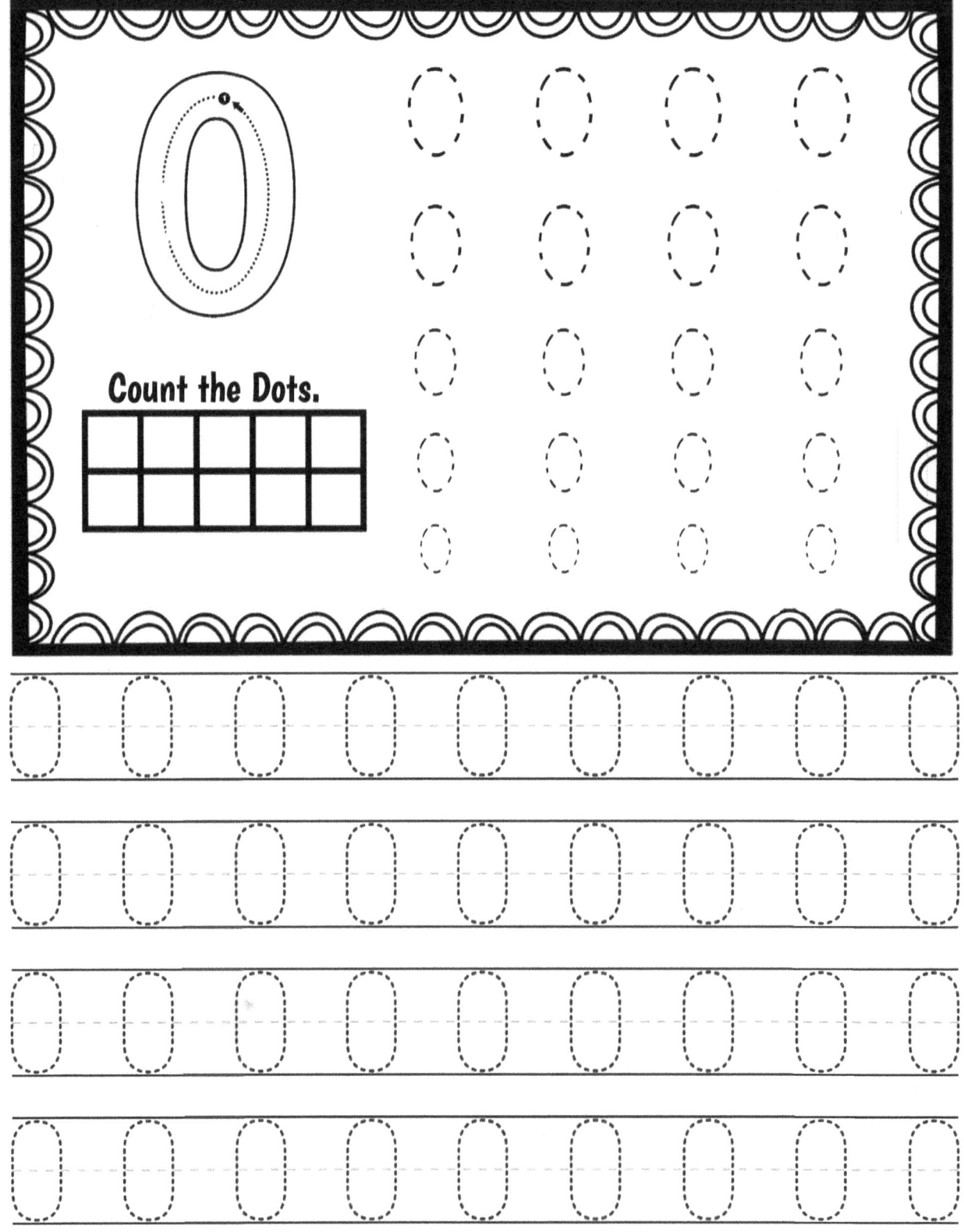

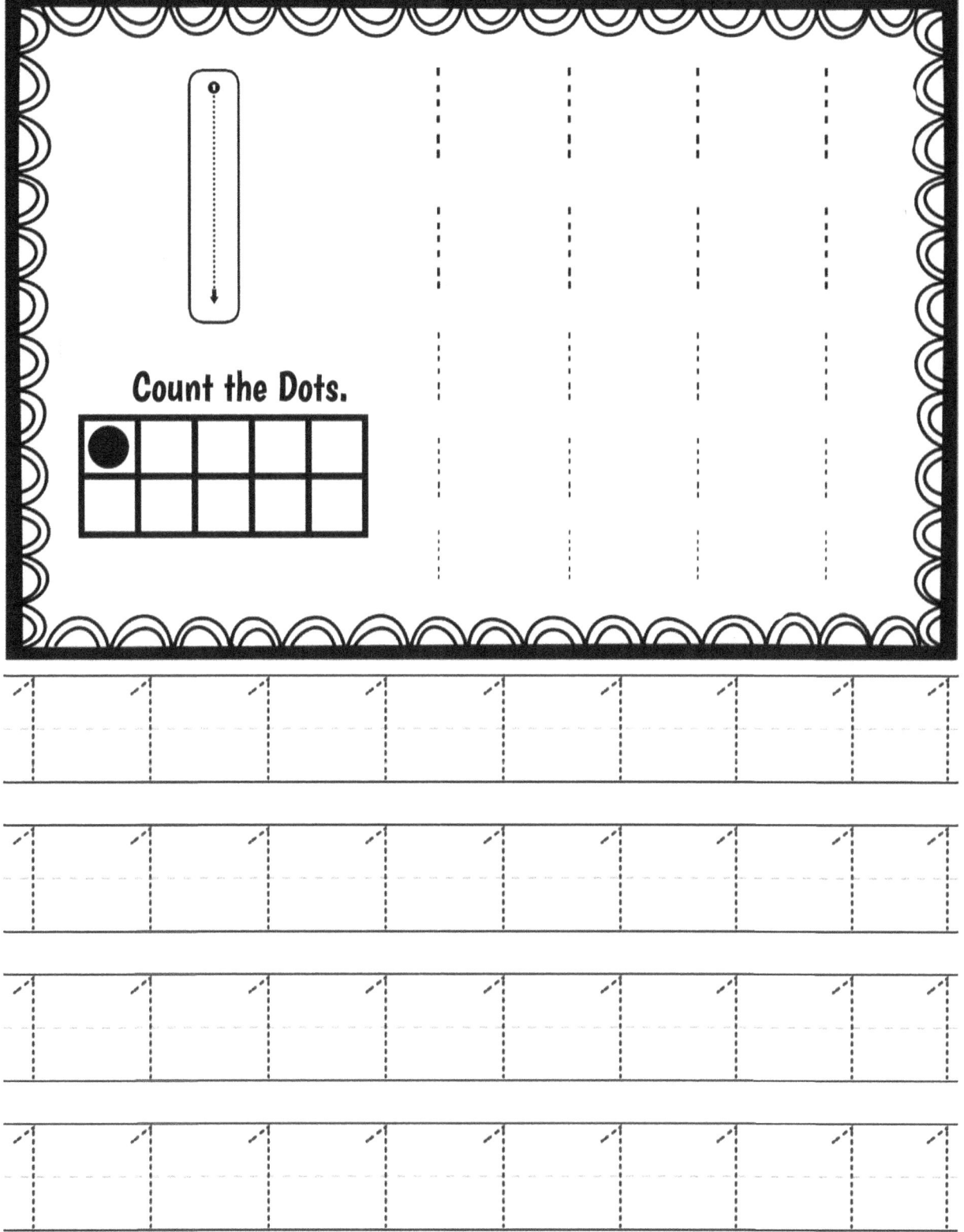

Tracing Numbers
Trace the numbers to complete the series.

Tracing Numbers
Trace the numbers to complete the series.

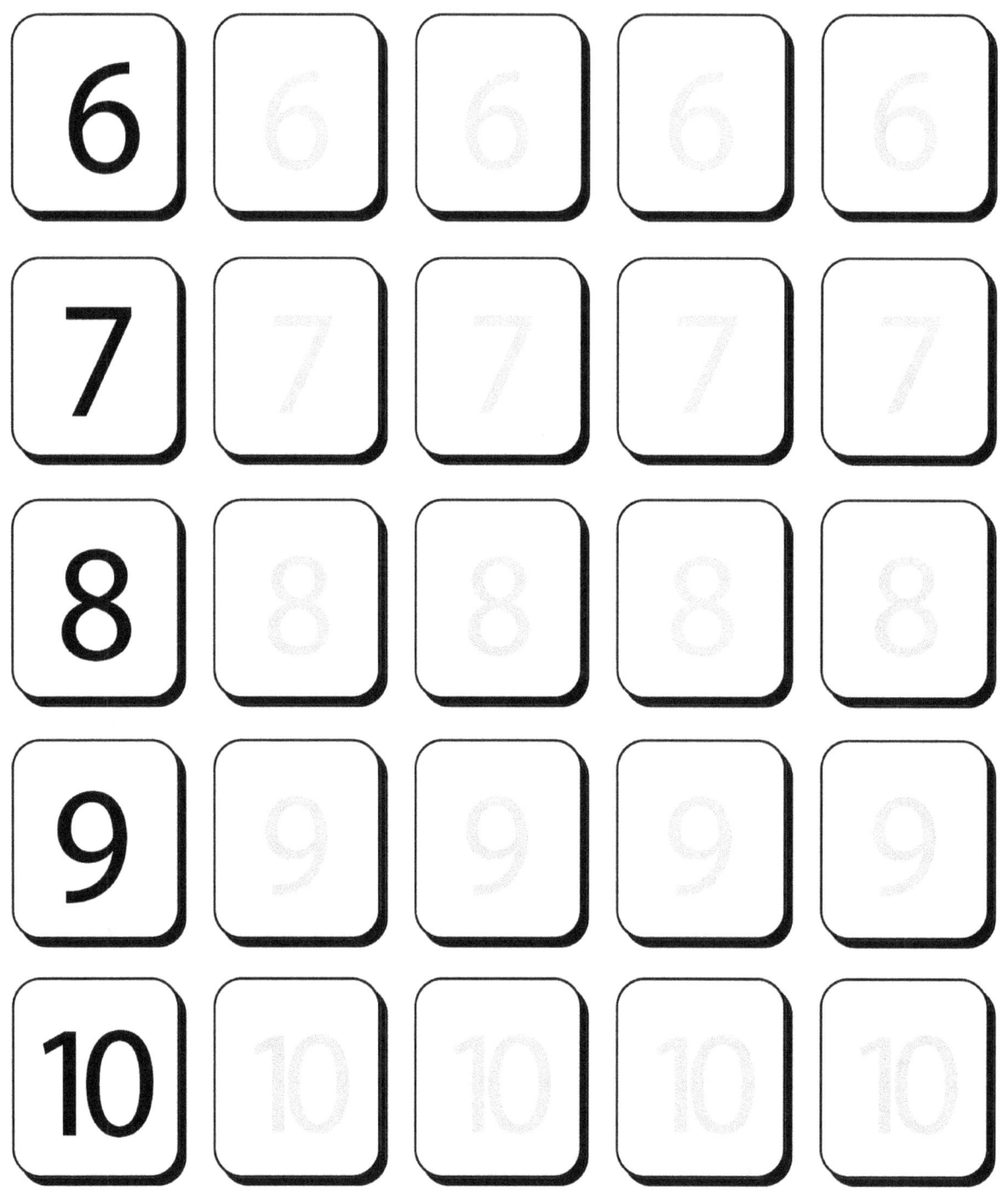

Teen Numbers
Write the teen numbers 11 - 15

Teen Numbers
Write the teen numbers 15 - 20

16 16 _____

17 17 _____

18 18 _____

19 19 _____

20 20 _____

Trace the numbers.

Writing Numbers Practice
Trace each number 2 or 3 times.
Begin at the correct starting point!

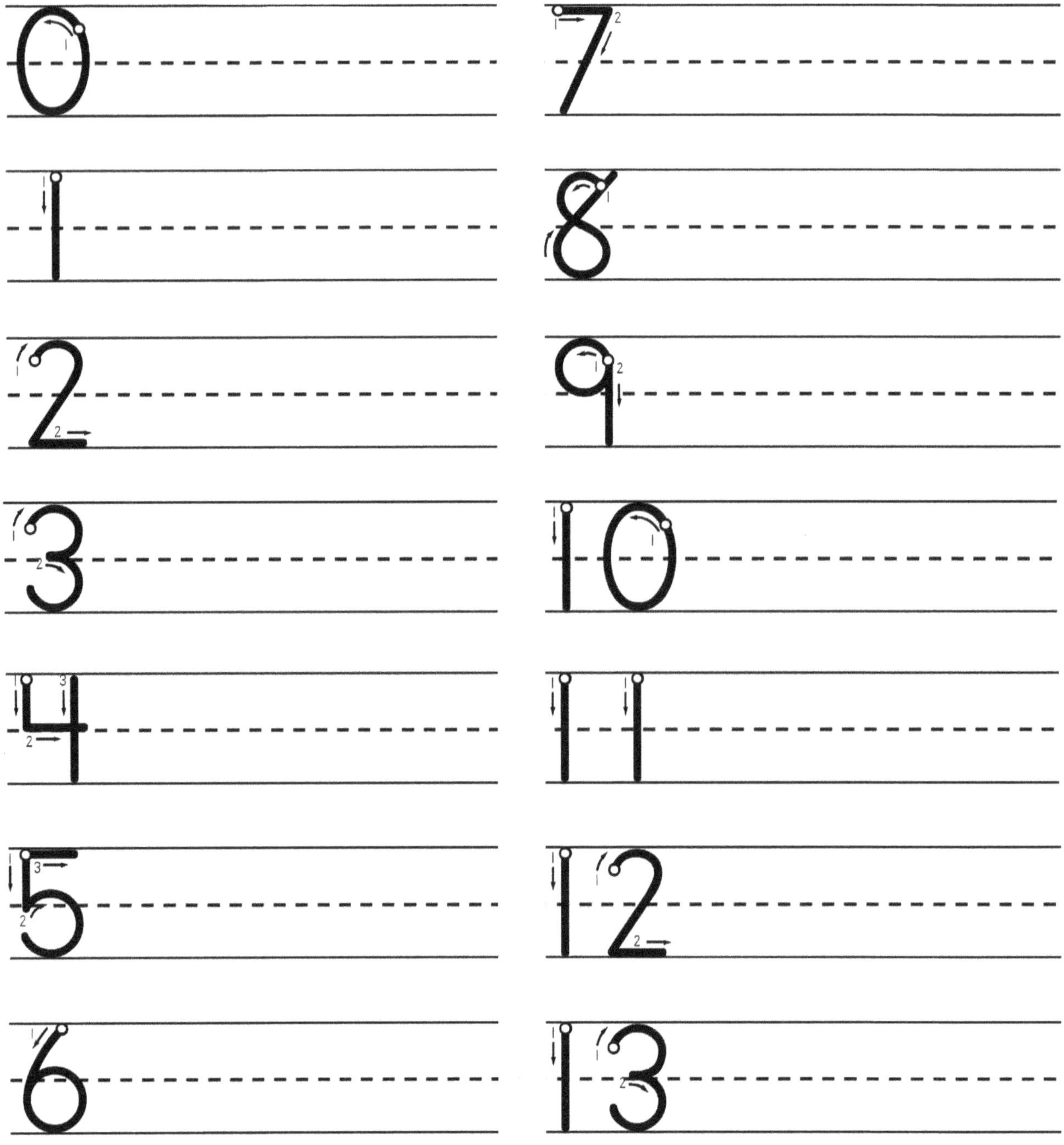

0

1

2

3

4

5

6

7

8

9

10

11

12

13

Writing Numbers Practice
Trace each number 2 or 3 times.
Begin at the correct starting point!

14 — 21

15 — 22

16 — 23

17 — 24

18 — 25

19 — 26

20 — 27

Writing Numbers Practice
Trace each number 2 or 3 times.
Begin at the correct starting point!

28   35

29   36

30   37

31   38

32   39

33   40

34   41

Writing Numbers Practice
Trace each number 2 or 3 times.
Begin at the correct starting point!

42   49
43   50
44   51
45   52
46   53
47   54
48   55

Writing Numbers Practice
Trace each number 2 or 3 times.
Begin at the correct starting point!

56   63

57   64

58   65

59   66

60   67

61   68

62   69

Writing Numbers Practice
Trace each number 2 or 3 times.
Begin at the correct starting point!

70   77
71   78
72   79
73   80
74   81
75   82
76   83

84	91
85	92
86	93
87	94
88	95
89	96
90	97

Trace each number 1 - 33.
Begin at the correct starting point!

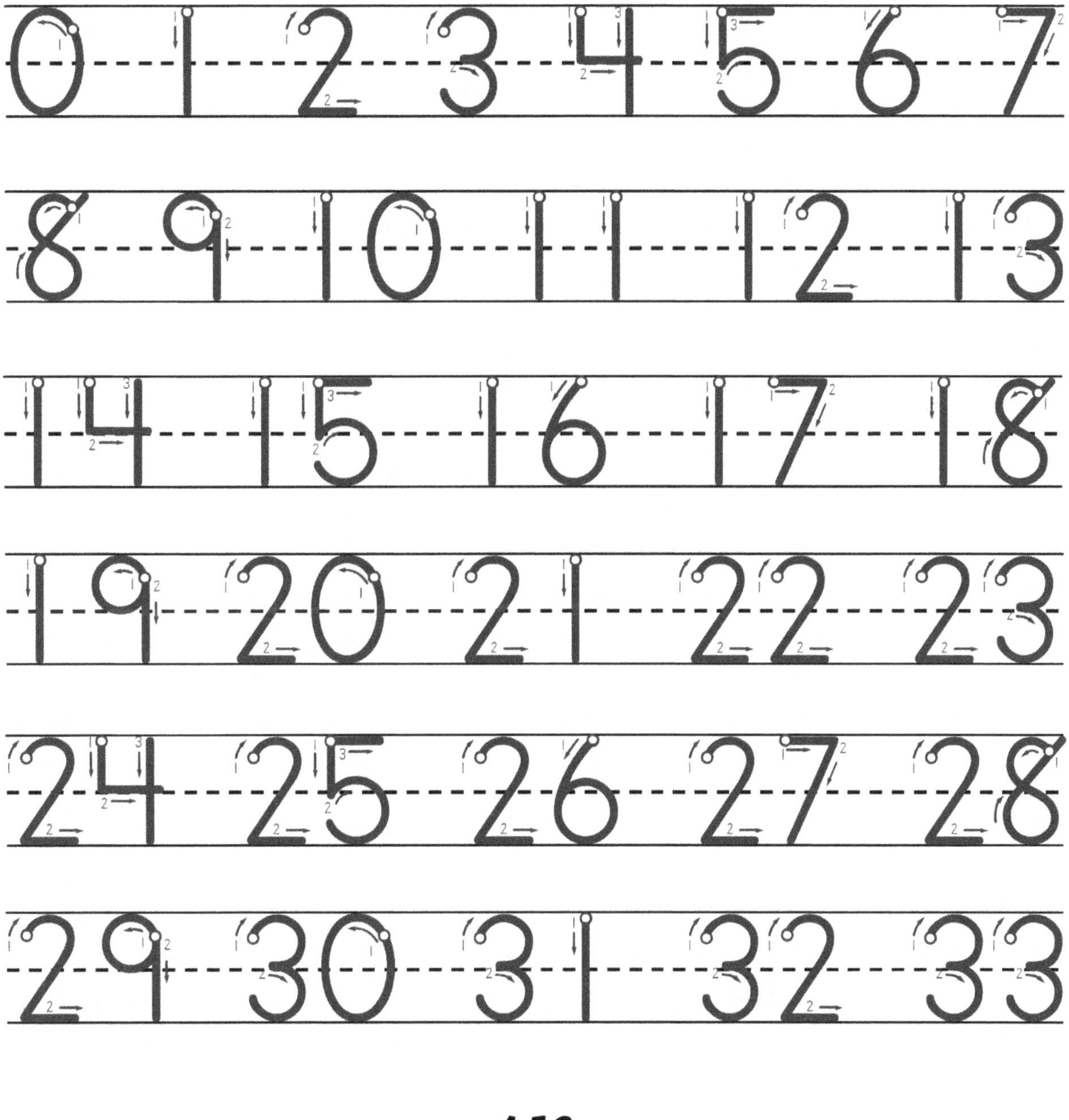

0 1 2 3 4 5 6 7

8 9 10 11 12 13

14 15 16 17 18

19 20 21 22 23

24 25 26 27 28

29 30 31 32 33

**Trace each number 34 - 63.
Begin at the correct starting point!**

34 35 36 37 38

39 40 41 42 43

44 45 46 47 48

49 50 51 52 53

54 55 56 57 58

59 60 61 62 63

64 65 66 67 68

69 70 71 72 73

74 75 76 77 78

79 80 81 82 83

84 85 86 87 88

89 90 91 92 93

94 95 96 97 98

99 100

Numbers 1-50
Fill in the Missing Numbers

1		3	4	
	7	8		10
11	12		14	15
16			19	
	22	23		25
26		28		30
31	32			35
36		38	39	
	42			45
46		48		50

Numbers 51-100
Fill in the Missing Numbers

51		53		55
56	57		59	
		63		65
	67		69	
71	72			75
		78	79	
81		83		85
86		88		
	92		94	95
96		98		100

NUMBERS 1-50
Fill in the Missing Numbers

1				
				50

NUMBERS 51-100
Fill in the Missing Numbers

51				
				100

Learn your number words
1 - 10

1		one
2		two
3		three
4		four
5		five
6		six
7		seven
8		eight
9		nine
10		ten

Write Your Number Word

Write Your Number Word

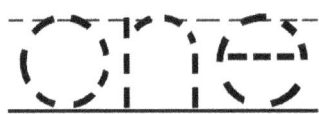

Write Your Number Word

Write Your Number Word

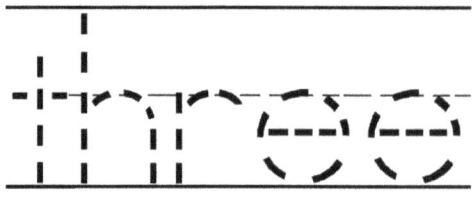

Write Your Number Word

_____

Write Your Number Word

Write Your Number Word

six

Write Your Number Word

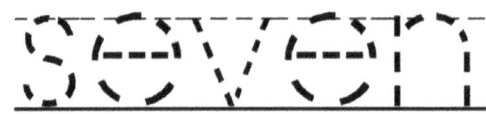

Write Your Number Word

Write Your Number Word

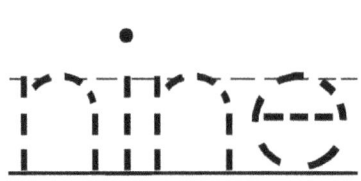

Write Your Number Word

ten

Write Your Number Word

Write Your Number Word

Color by Number

Use the color key below to reveal the beautiful butterfly.

1 = Green
2 = Orange
3 = Brown
4 = Blue
5 = Purple
6 = Yellow

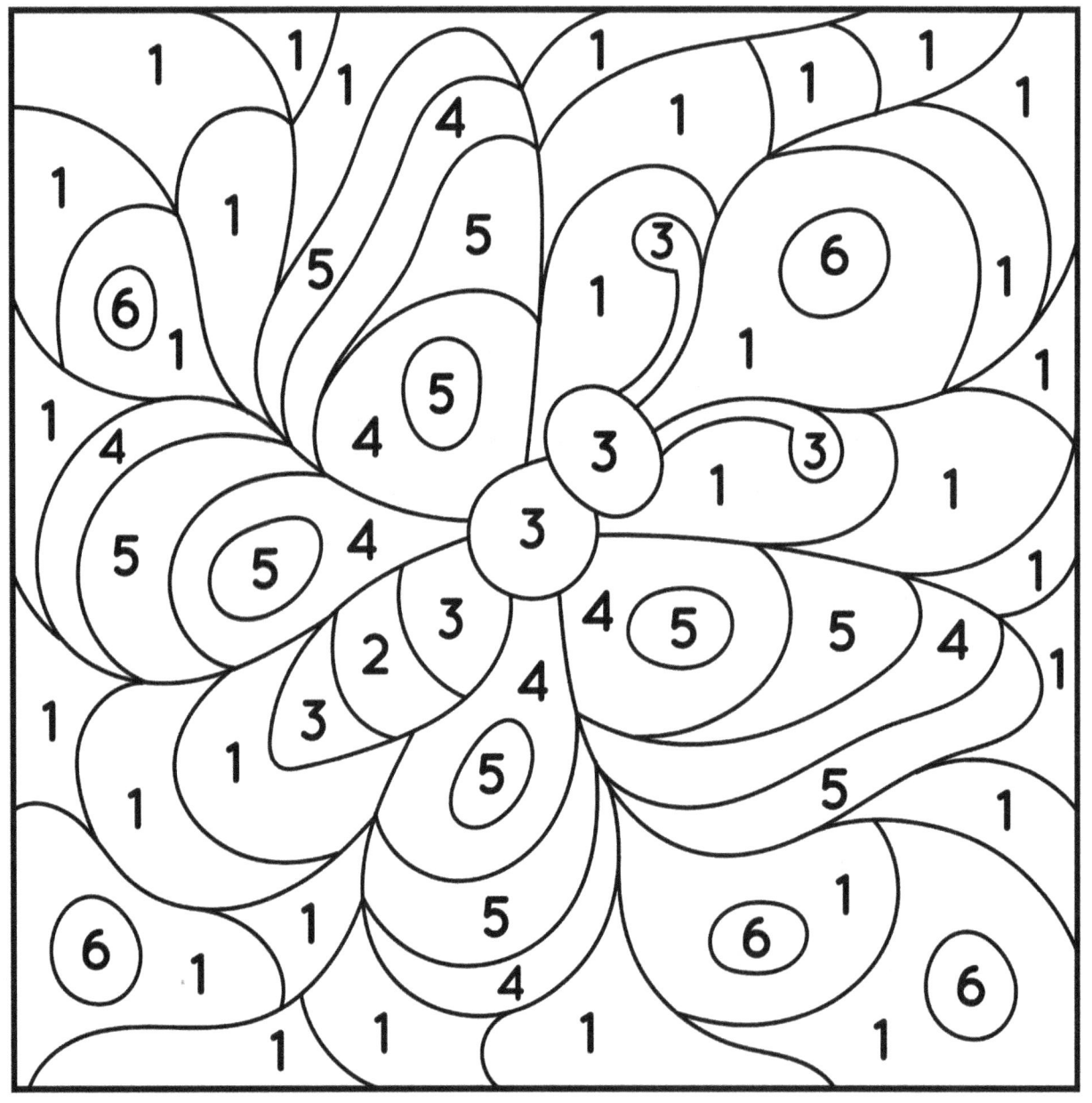

Color by Number

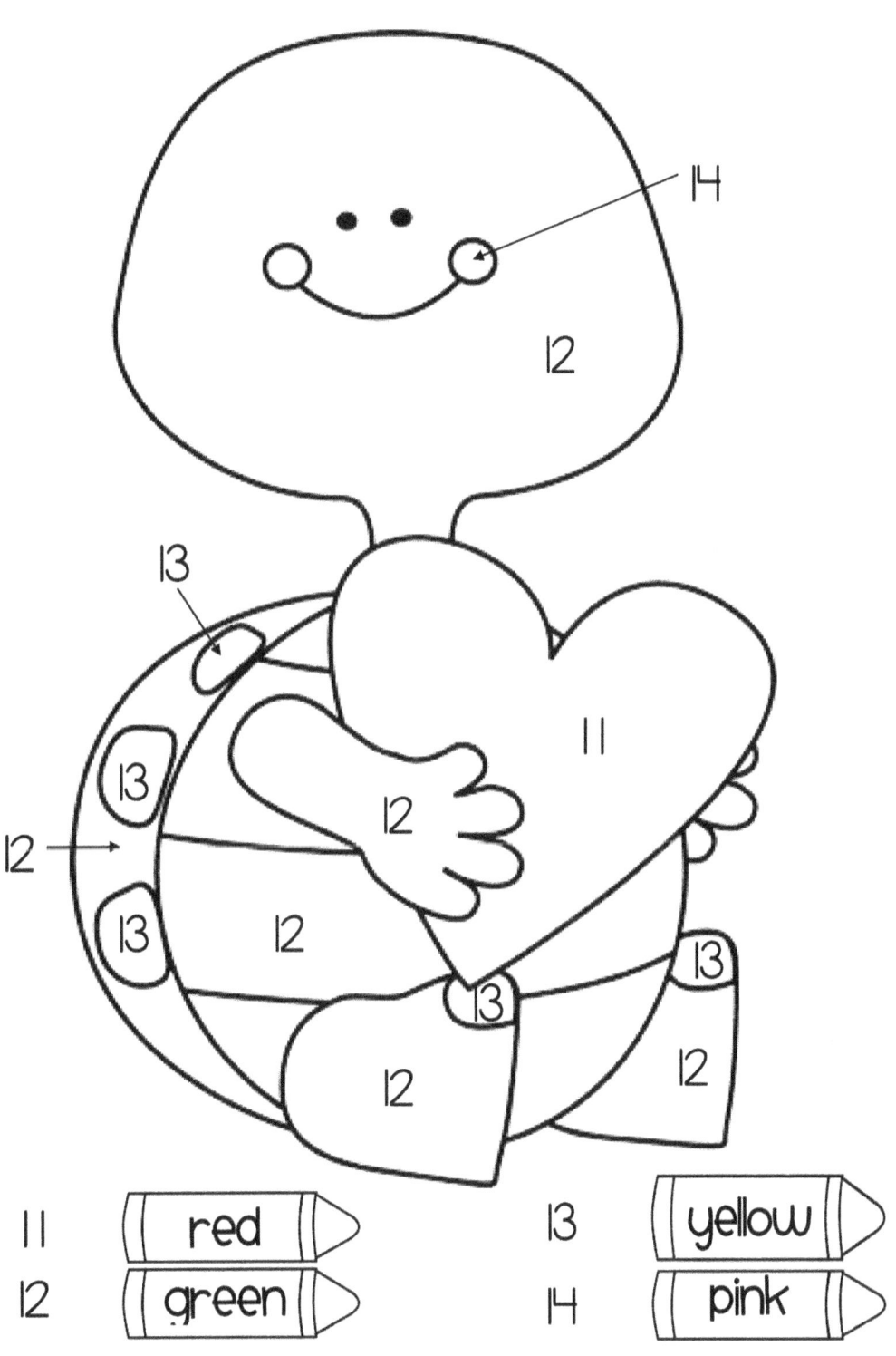

Color by Number

Color by Number Word

0-green   6-orange

1-blue   7 - brown

2-red   8 - black

3 - yellow   9 - pink

4 - white

5-purple

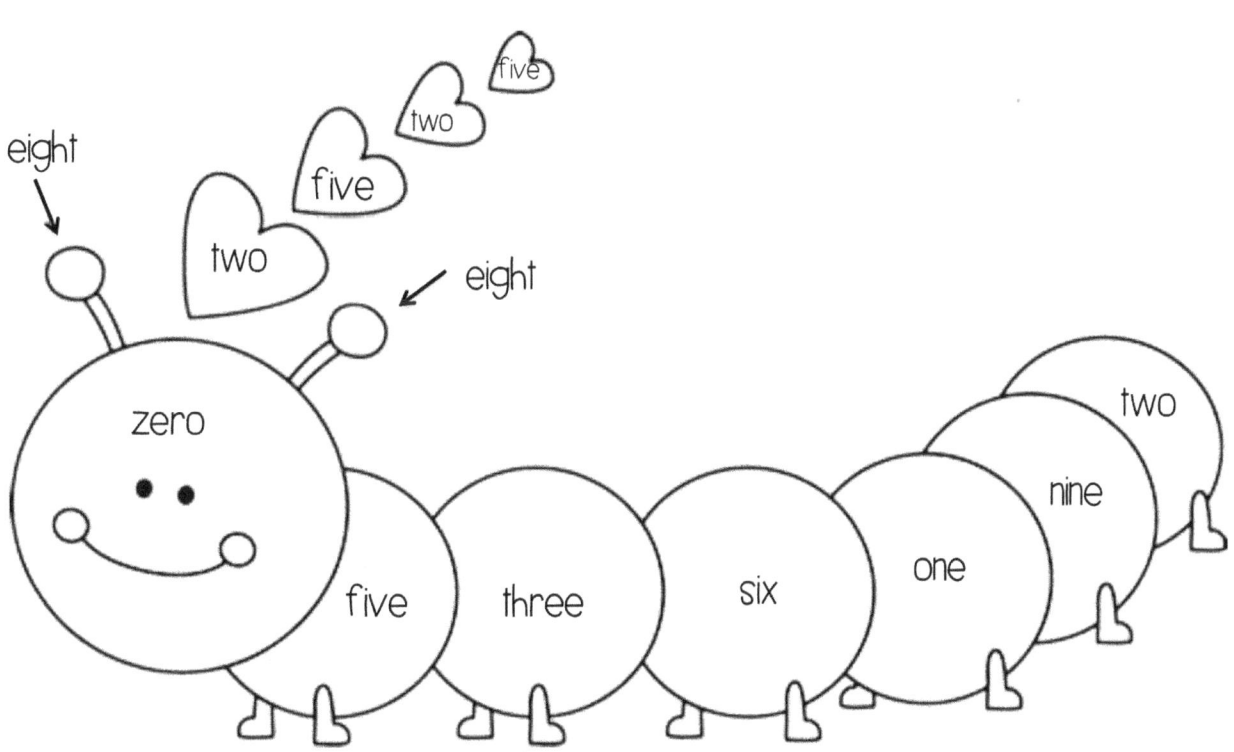

Under the Sea
Color and Count — Numbers 1-5

How many?

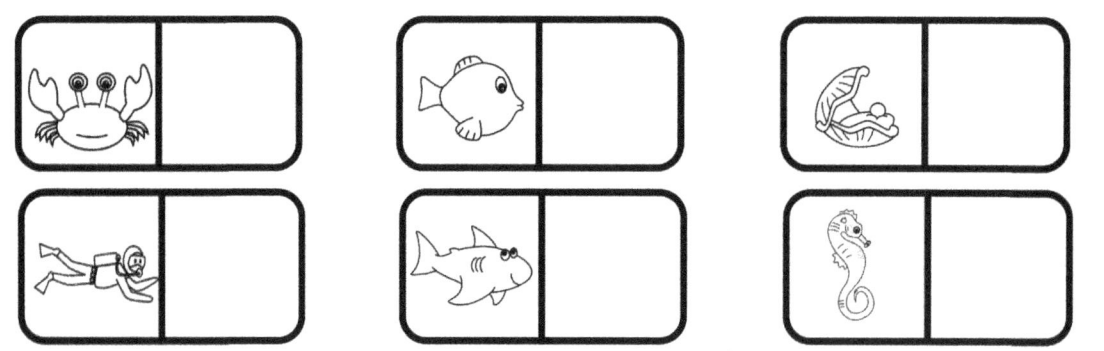

Under the Sea
Color and Count — Numbers 5-10

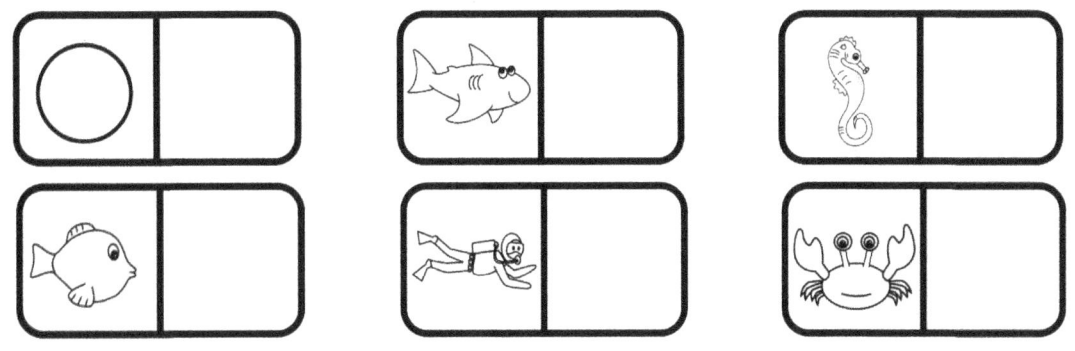

How many?

Color by Number

1 = Green   2 = Orange   5 = Blue   6 = Pink
3 = Brown   4 = Yellow   7 = Gray   8 = Purple

Shapes and Colors

The three basic shapes are a square, a triangle and a circle. All other shapes are derived from these. The four easiest shapes to learn are circle, square, triangle, and star.

Practice tracing the shapes. Then color them all in.

Practice tracing the shapes. Then color them all in.

I LOVE SHAPES!

Shape the maze: follow the △'s to find the path to the hole in the ice.

Shape the maze: follow the ◯'s to help the bear get back to his cave.

Shape It Up!
Can you write each shape with its name?

Square
Heart
Star
Circle
Triangle

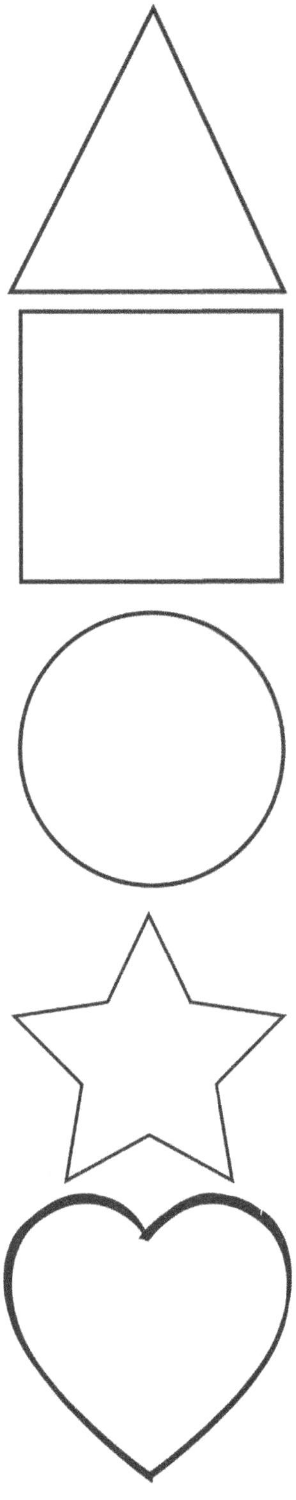

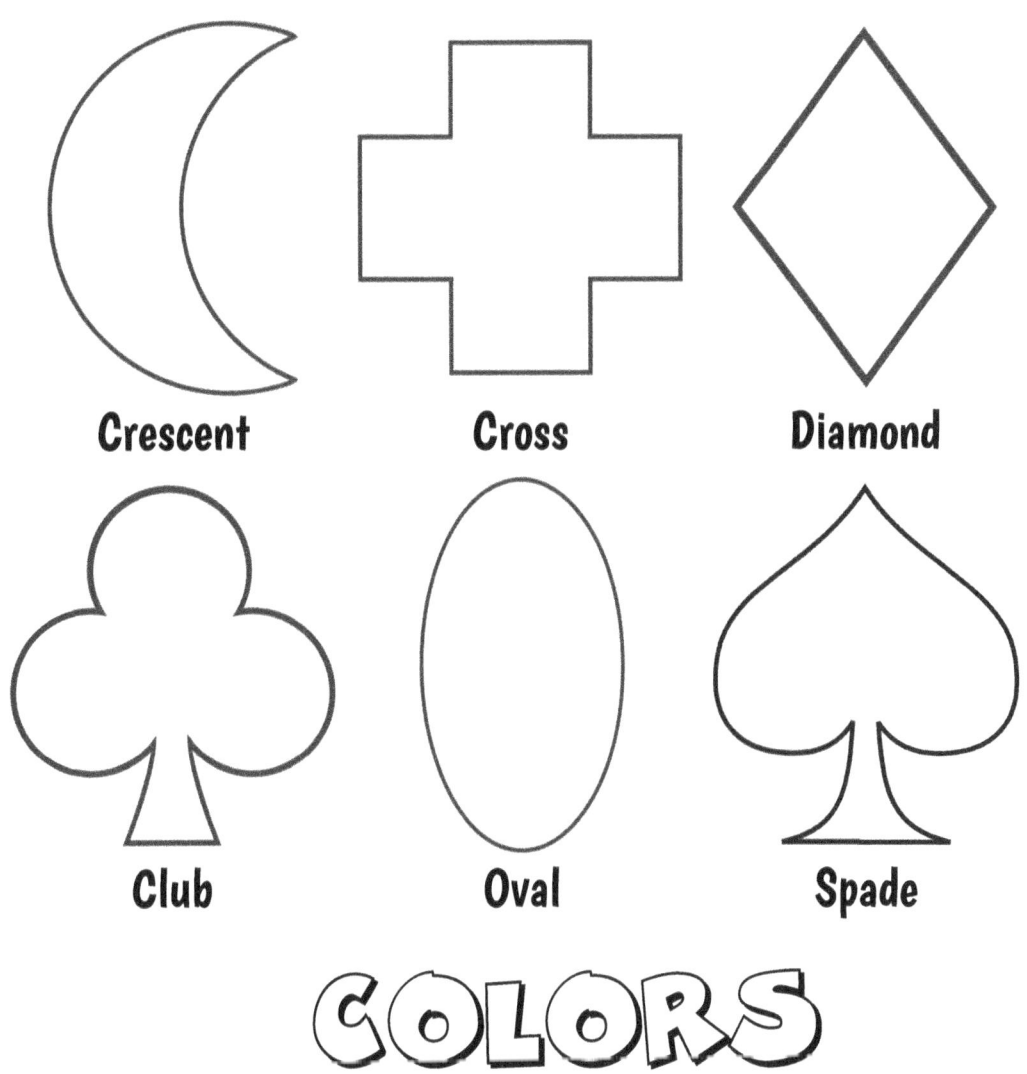

Crescent Cross Diamond

Club Oval Spade

COLORS

One way to teach students about color is to pick a new color each week and completely focus on that color with your food choices, activities, etc. Introduce the primary colours, red, yellow, and blue and explain a little about them. Do this for the rest of the colors.

By the end of the year, students should be able to not only match rainbow colors, (red, yellow, green, orange, purple, blue) but spell all eleven basic colors as well — including brown, black, white, gray, and pink.

Color Words
My Brain is Ready to Grow!

Name: ....

I Know My Colors

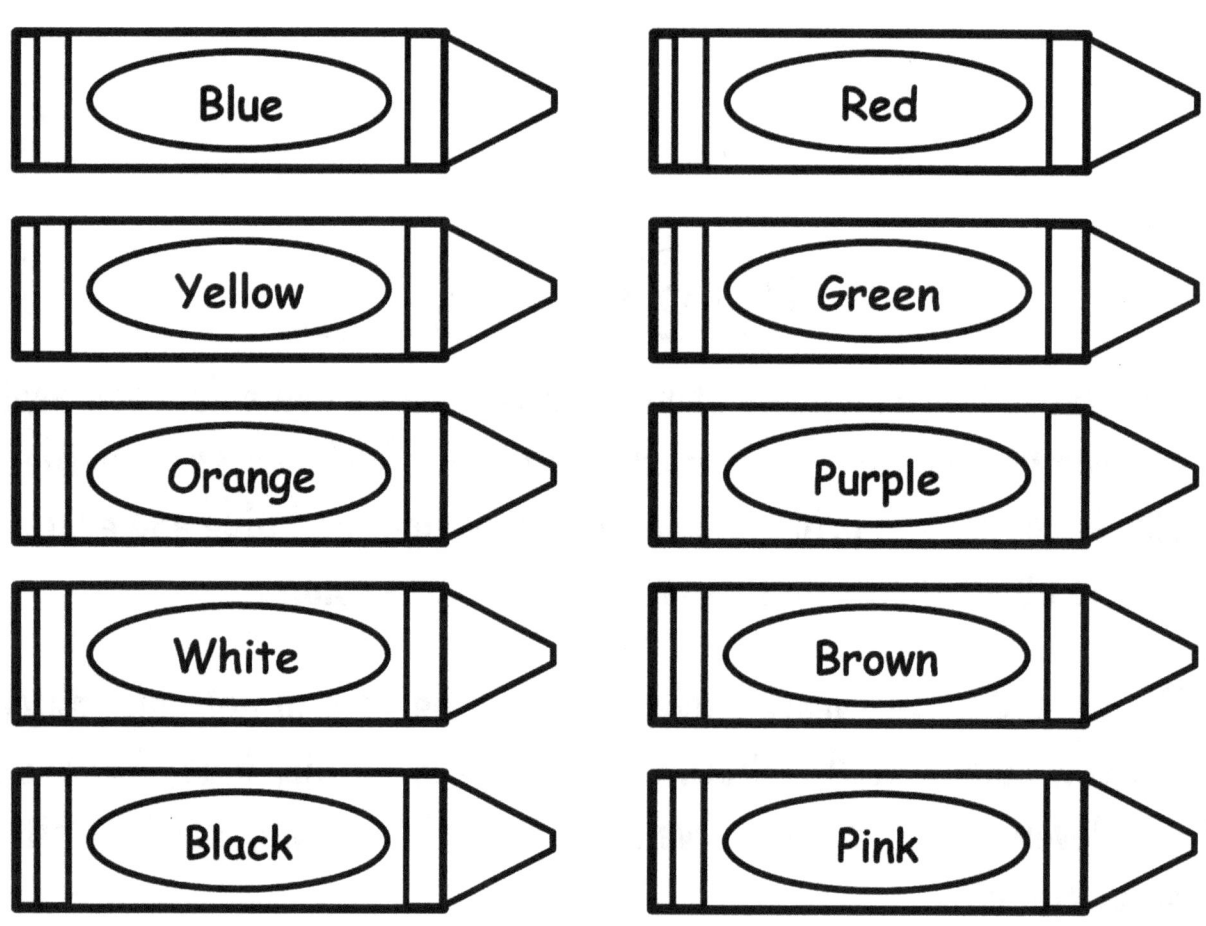

- Blue
- Yellow
- Orange
- White
- Black
- Red
- Green
- Purple
- Brown
- Pink

What is red?
Complete each color word:

These things are red.

strawberry

red

tomato

_ed

ladybug

__d

___

apple

Name:

Color 5 things that are red.

**What is yellow?
Complete each color word:**

These things are yellow.

yellow

__ellow

__llow

__low

__ow

__w

banana

corn

lemon

sun

egg yoke

Name: _____

Color 5 things that are yellow.

What is green?
Complete each color word:

These things are green.

alligator

green

__reen

__een

__en

__n

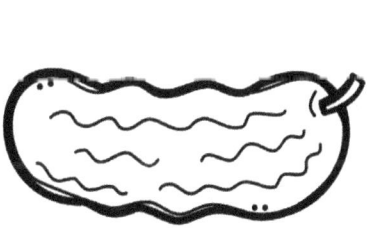
turtle

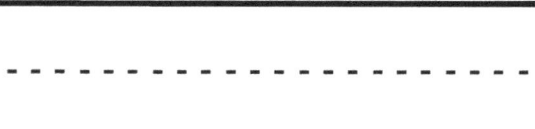
pickle

cactus

frog

Name:

Color 5 things that are green.

What is blue?
Complete each color word:

blue

__lue

__ue

__e

_____

These things are blue.

blueberries

bluejay

blue jeans

handicap sign

sky

Name:

Color 5 things that are blue.

Name:

Color 5 things that are white.

What is orange?
Complete each color word:

These things are orange.

orange

___range

___ange

___nge

___ge

___e

orange

carrot

pumpkin

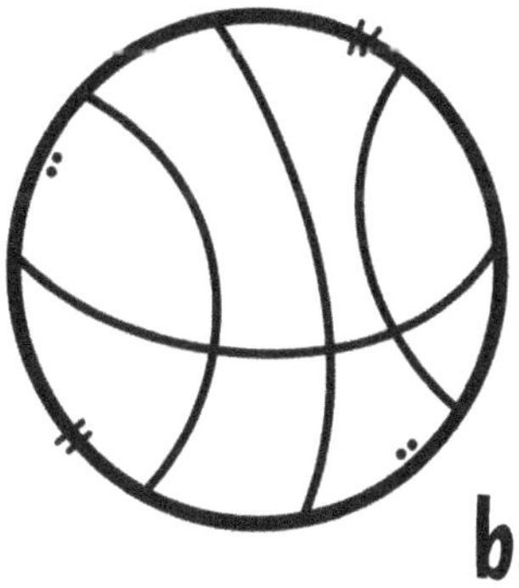

basketball

goldfish

Name:

Color 5 things that are orange.

What is brown?
Complete each color word:

brown

__rown

__own

__wn

__n

_____

These things are brown.

squirrel

bear

log

acorn
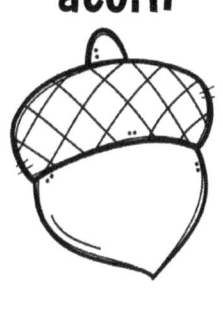

mortar & pestle

Name: ....

Color 5 things that are brown.

**What is gray?
Complete each color word:**

These things are gray.

gray

_ray

_ _ay

_ _ _y

_ _ _ _

shark

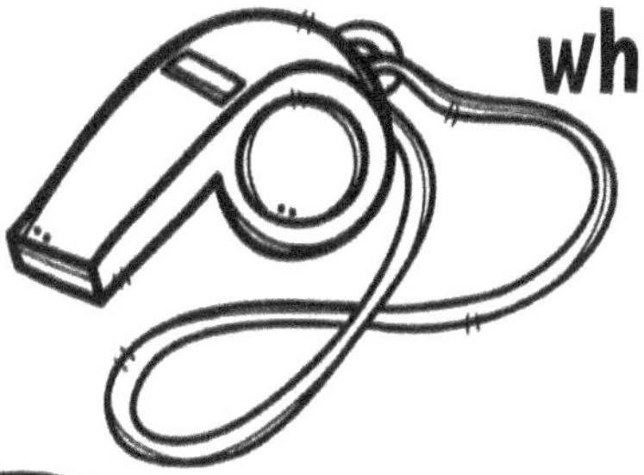

whistle

coin

elephant

whale

Name: _____

Color 5 things that are gray.

What is purple?
Complete each color word:

These things are purple.

purple

___urple

___rple

___ple

___le

___e

grape jam

African violet

plum

eggplant

grapes

Name: _____

Color 5 things that are purple.

206

What is pink?
Complete each color word:

pink

_ink

_nk

___k

____

These things are pink.

bubblegum

pig

flamingoes

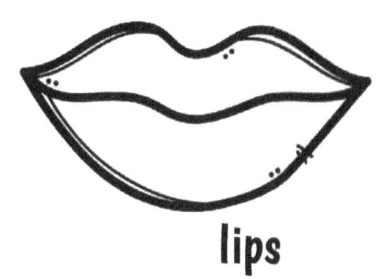
lips

Name: ....

Color 5 things that are pink.

What is black?
Complete each color word:

black

_lack

__ack

___ck

____k

_____

These things are black.

bat

penguin

hat

skunk

spider

Name: ....

Color 5 things that are black.

Name: ....

Use the color code to color the picture.

1- red 5- black
2- green 6- yellow
3- pink 7- brown
4- blue

Mixing Some Colors

Now that we have learn our colors, let's try mixing some secondary colors by mixing the primary colors together!
1 - Blue
2 - Yellow
3 - Red
4 - Green
5 - Orange
6 - Purple
What happens when you mix all three of the primary colors?
7- Mystery color!

PRIMARY + PRIMARY = SECONDARY

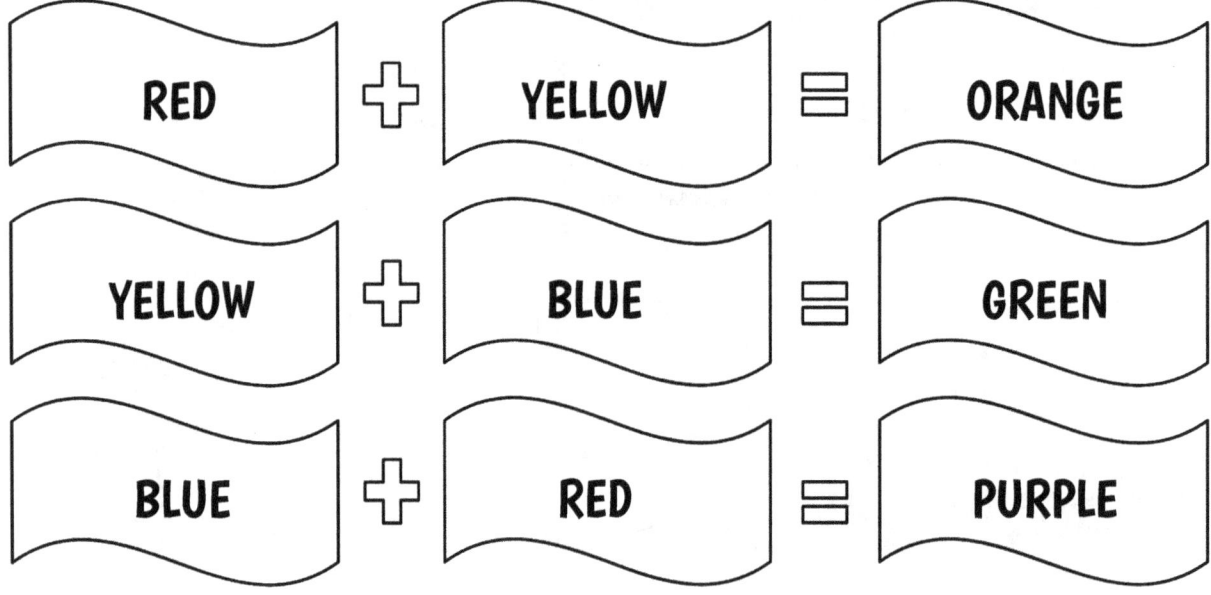

The future of the world is in this classroom!

Teach your students about a growth mindset this year.

Growth Mindset — what is it?

We used to think that our intelligence was fixed — meaning we were either smart or we weren't. Scientists have proven again and again that simply is not true. Our brain acts like a muscle — the more we use it, the stronger (and smarter) our brain becomes.

THE BRAIN CAN GROW!
Teach your students how to grow their brains!

 Inspire your students to adopt a growth mindset. Learners should be encouraged to aim for the "normal" to "kind of hard" range to raise progress. Whenever they say, "This is so hard!" Remember, tell them that it's always hard at first. Every day you do it, it gets less hard and a little more normal, and a little more comfortable until you finally begin to feel like you know what you're doing or know what you're talking about. The first step in the continuum of learning is accepting that "This is hard!" is ok and normal when it's new. The next step is to tell yourself, "I can do hard things." And next, tell yourself, "I'm right where I'm supposed to be." This works for all humans, big and small. Help your students understand the differences between a "fixed" mindset and a "growth" mindset.

What is a "Growth Mindset?"

Growth mindset is believing that your brain can grow and you can learn many new things. You are not born smart; you become smart. People believe that their most basic abilities can be developed through dedication and hard work—brains and talent are just the starting point. This view creates a love of learning and a resilience that is essential for great accomplishment.

Fixed Mindset

A fixed mindset is quite the opposite. It is believing that you cannot learn new things. Remind your students that their intelligence is not fixed. Remind them that when things are difficult, their brain grows if they persists through the challenge. Each time they learn something new, their brain is making new connections. Your students need to know this is possible!

For students at this level, teach them that a growth mindset is believing in the power of yourself and your brain!

Growth Mindset vs Fixed Mindset

A person with a fixed mindset may do these things:
- avoid challenges
- give up easily
- ignore feedback
- become threatened by other people's success
- try hard to appear as smart or capable as possible

A person with a growth mindset may do these things:
- embrace challenges
- give their best effort
- learn from feedback
- become inspired by other people's successes
- believe their intelligence can change if they work hard

Growth Mindset	Fixed Mindset
Loves challenges	Avoids challenges
Listens to feedbacks	Gives up easily
Learns from mistakes	Avoids making mistakes
Instrested in learning	Ignores feedbacks

Encourage a Growth Mindset in your class. If a student says, "This is too hard!" Help them change that to "I can't do this yet, but I will keep trying." Give them the words to say when they are feeling defeated.

Let the students repeat this in your class before each lesson starts:

My Brain is Strong!
I can do this!

Giving feedback to a student.

Feedback is passing on information to someone about their behavior, actions, or performance. How do you explain feedback to a child? The goal should always be to provide sensible and related ideas and suggestions for improvement. Make sure it is helpful information or criticism that is given to say what can be done to improve performance. It is most productive for students' learning when they are provided with an explanation of what is accurate and inaccurate about their work. Providing feedback means giving students an explanation of what they are doing correctly AND incorrectly, with the focus of the feedback on what the students are doing right.

When giving students feedback, keep these tips in mind:
1. **Praise their efforts, not their talents.** Try using praise like "I am so proud of all the effort you put into this," or "All your hard work really paid off."
2. **Mistakes and errors don't need to feel negative.** Mistakes are part of the learning process, and that real learning can't happen without them. The only true failure can come if you quit!
3. **Be specific.** Offering feedback detailing exactly what students are doing well, or what they need to improve upon.
4. **Explain feedback wherever possible.** Offer detailed explanations of why you chose to make those suggestions.
5. **Start with a clear goal.** If students know where they're headed from the start, they will more easily be able to check back in during the process to make sure they're on track.
6. **Keep it timely.** Feedback is most valuable when it is given immediately following the task, or even during the process of completing it. The longer you wait between students' activities and giving your feedback on it, the less relevant your comments become. Whenever possible, try to engage in feedback as students are working, or as soon as possible.
7. **Feedback isn't just for finished work.** Many teachers only provide feedback at the end of a completed task—after a test, an essay, a project, and so on. But the most effective feedback is actually given during the creation process, because

it gives students the chance to shift and pivot their work in the moment. Try to be present to offer feedback to students throughout every step of the process, so they can put your suggestions into practice right away.

8. Give feedback one-on-one. The best feedback is given on a personalized, individual level, rather than as addressed to an entire group. By offering personal, one-on-one feedback, you're showing your students that you're aware of what they're doing on an individual level, and that you're there to support them.

9. Allow time for questions and discussion. By offering students a chance to ask questions about feedback, we can give them an opportunity to understand it with greater depth.

10. Teach students how to give (and recognize) useful feedback. By teaching students to give quality feedback to their peers, you're also showing them what quality feedback looks like when it's coming back to them.

How to explain the meaning of "challenge" to young students.

Explain that challenge is something that needs great mental or physical effort in order to be done successfully and therefore tests a person's ability. For a student, a challenge is something new and difficult which requires great effort and determination, like learning the ABCs for the first time. The best word to use so that they understand what challenge means is "hard". A challenge is something that puts you to the test.

A student with a growth mindset will accept the challenge to learn the alphabet. It may be hard, but they will be willing to try until they learn.

THE BRAIN CAN GROW!

Growth mindset quotes to use for kids.

Growth mindset quotes for students can be both motivational and inspirational and can help them move forward when they feel stuck. Having a growth mindset encourages kids to keep trying, to work on their skills, to be positive and solution focussed and to not feel defeated or give up.

1. It does not matter how slowly you go so long as you do not stop.
2. You have not failed unless you have quit trying.
3. Attitude is a little thing that makes a big difference.
4. Nothing is impossible. The word itself says 'I'm Possible!'
5. Always do what you are afraid of doing.
6. It's not that I'm so smart. It's just that I stay with problems longer.
7. Believe in yourself.
8. Be positive
9. Smart is something you become, not something you are.
10. Just do it!
11. I can do hard things.
12. Made a mistake? Try again.
13. You can train your brain to figure it out.
14. Mistakes are proof that you are trying.
15. Practice makes progress.

Teaching growth mindset to young students
Having a growth mindset.

Instead of saying . . .	Try thinking . . .
I'm not good at this.	What am I missing?
I'm awesome at this.	I'm on the right track!
I give up.	I will use some of the tactics we have learned.
This is too hard.	This may take some time and effort.
I can't make this any better.	I can always improve so I will keep trying.
I just can't do Math.	I am going to train my brain in Math.
I made a mistake.	Mistakes help me to learn better.
That other boy/girl is so smart. I will never be smart.	I am going to figure out how he/she does it, so I can try it with some more effort!
It is good enough.	Is it really my best work?

Character Building

Character Education (also known as social skills) are skills we need to teach just like we teach letters and sounds. It is a life skill! Most of us take basic social skills for granted because we learned them when we were young and use them daily. Social skills are important to any child's future success in school and life.

Teachers should create a classroom of confident students who can solve problems, make good choices, be kind to others, and follow routines using good character traits. Someone with good character believes they should make good choices and shows over time that they almost always make choices that are honest, respectful, fair, caring, and responsible. Making a mistake doesn't mean you don't have good character. It has been said that character can be measured by what one would do if no one were looking.

Why is good character important for children? It is also helpful to know why children need character traits in the first place. Not only do they empower children holistically, but they also help them deal with stressful situations. Positive character traits for children provide a guiding light to analyze emotions and understand situations better. Teaching character traits to our children is important, especially when they face trials.

A great way to teach good character to children is to teach them how to put good character qualities into practice. When helping children grow and change, we want to be practical with them. That means that we give specific instructions about what we want them to do, not just what they shouldn't do. One way to be practical as we help children develop character is to use working definitions.

Five Character Traits

The five character traits to encourage learning.

Acceptance - talk about acceptance with students; (a) What do they think acceptance means and why is it important? (b) Have them talk about someone who is different than they are. (c) How can differences be a good thing? (d) What is one way they can show acceptance at school? (e) Has anyone ever made them feel accepted? Have them talk about it. (f) What would the world look like if everyone was the same?

Together with the students, pick a few different foods, and try to eat them each with a spoon, knife and fork. Talk about what would happen if we only had forks? Knives? Spoons? Use this activity to talk about how our differences make a stronger community.

Honesty - Here are some discussion points to help you talk about honesty with students. (a) Has anyone ever been dishonest to them before? How did they feel? (b) What do they think honesty means and why is it important? (c) Have them tell you about a time when it was hard to be honest. (d) What makes it hard to be honest? (e) How will others view them if they are honest? How will others view them if they are dishonest? Help students learn the difference between a truth and a lie with this simple game.

You and students take turns saying statements and the other person has to decide if it is a truth or a lie.

Kindness - Here are some discussion points to help you talk about kindness with students: (a) Have them tell you about a time when someone was kind to them. How did it make them feel? (b) What do they think kindness means and why is it important? (c) Who is someone in the class they can be kind to? (d) What are ways they can be kind to people at home, at school and in the community? Spend time writing encouraging notes to each other.

Perseverance - Here are some discussion points to help you talk about perseverance with students: (a) What do they think perseverance means and why is it important? (b) Have them tell you about a time when it was hard to get through a challenge. How did they feel after? (c) What are some things that are hard for them to push through, and how can you help? (d) What are 3 goals they have? What may be some challenges to meeting these goals? What will happen if they don't give up? Help students learn to persevere by engaging in difficult tasks with each student. Find something to do together and commit to pushing each other through the challenge.

Responsibility - Here are some discussion points to help you talk about responsibility with students: (a) What do they think responsibility means and why is it important? (b) Have them tell you about a time when it was hard to be responsible. (c) What is a way they would like to have more responsibility at home? (d) What are their responsibilities in the classroom and in the community?

Help students practice responsibility by giving each student a special job! Let each student pick a special chore each week that they can be responsible for.

Being Independent

Working independently means you can do it by yourself. It is important for you to do things independently. This means you complete them by yourself. The teacher is here if you need him/her, but you should also try to figure it out by yourself first. It will make you feel good about yourself when you can complete it on your own.

Responsible for Items — take care of your school supplies, don't be wasteful with your supplies and other things. Situations of being wasteful could be taking more food at lunch than you will eat, throwing away paper that could still be used, or throwing away a glue stick that is not empty yet. Some examples of not being wasteful could be saving half a sandwich for later or using the back of a paper to draw a picture. Clean up after yourself and help others. Be more responsible for your items by keeping track of them and knowing where you put them.

Being a Leader and not a follower — it is better to be a leader and lead people to do the right thing, than to be a follower following someone who is doing the wrong thing; doing the right thing for NO reward, and thinking of others before yourself.

Introducing Oneself

Review how the student is to introduce themselves to someone new. Have them repeat the phrase, "Hello, my name is _____."

Good Character Vocabulary

Definations students can easily understand.	
Collaboration	To work well with others, by contributing in a respectful and productive way.
Compassion	To show care and empathy for someone. To treat someone kindly and with love.
Compromise	An agreement that is reached by each side making a decision.
Confidence	To feel certain (positive).
Courage	A feeling of bravery and strength.
Creativity	To use your imagination and think outside the box.
Curiosity	A strong desire to learn or know something new.
Diligence	To show careful and persistent work or effort.
Empathy	The ability to understand and share the feelings of another.
Enthusiasm	To express pure joy and excitement.
Flexibility	The willingness to change and make compromises.
Forgiveness	To let go of bad feelings and to stop feeling upset toward someone for a problem or mistake.
Friendship	To share trust in another person and to share positive experiences together.
Generosity	Showing kindness and a readiness to give more of something than is expected.
Gratitude	To feel thankful and show appreciation for the people and things in your life
Grit	To show the strength of character. To have courage and persistence.
Honesty	To tell the truth, no matter what.
Hope	To feel positive about an outcome.

Definations students can easily understand.

Humility	To restrain from showing too much pride. To restrain from showing off or boasting.
Independence	To work on your own, without much direction or supervision.
Integrity	To be honest and to do the right thing, because it's the right thing to do.
Joy	A feeling of happiness.
Kindness	The quality of being friendly, generous, and considerate.
Leadership	To show influence over a group of people.
Love	A feeling of affection and admiration.
Loyalty	To show strong support.
Mindfulness	To be aware of yourself and your surroundings.
Obedience	To show compliance with a rule or request.
Optimism	To feel hopeful about the future. To look on the bright side.
Patience	To accept or tolerate when things aren't comfortable without getting upset.
Peace	A feeling of calm and freedom from disturbance.
Perseverance	To keep trying, even when something is really hard.
Resilience	To recover quickly from difficult moments and keep trying over and over again.
Resourcefulness	The ability to find quick and clever ways to overcome difficulties.
Respect	A feeling of deep admiration for someone or something.
Responsibility	To show ownership and independence.
Self-Control	The ability to control your feelings, especially in difficult situations.
Self-discipline	Putting off present rewards for future benefits.

Definations students can easily understand.	
Tolerance	To accept when things look or feel different. To be open-minded to differences.
Trustworthiness	The ability to be relied on with honesty or trust.
Zest	To show great enthusiasm and positive energy for something.

Good Manners Alphabet

A great citizen has good manners, from A to Z.

I can learn my good manner alphabets.	
A	Arrive On Time.
B	Be patient.
C	Close Doors Quietly.
D	Don't Pout.
E	Elbows Off Table.
F	Finders Are Not Keepers.
G	Go To Bed Without Fussing.
H	Hand Stuff Over.
I	Interrupting Is Not Nice.
J	Jokes Should Not Hurt Others.

	I can learn my good manner alphabets.
K	Knock And Wait to hear, "Come In."
L	Listen Closely.
M	"May I?" Is A Good Way To Ask.
N	No Hats At The Table, Please.
O	Obey Rules.
P	Pay Attention to details.
Q	Quit Wanting To Be First.
R	Role-model Kindness To Others.
S	Share Your Toys.
T	"Thank You" and "Please" Are Good Courtesies.
U	Use Positive Words.
V	Views of Others Must Be Handled Tenderly.
W	Wait Your Turn.
X	"eXcuse me, please," is a key phrase.
Y	"Yes" sounds better than "yep" or "yeah."
Z	Zoom! Zoom! is for outdoors!

52 Bible Verses to Memorize

Acts 16:31 Believe in the Lord Jesus Christ, and you will be saved.	**1 John 4:19** We love because he first loved us.	**Proverbs 14:5** A honest witness does not lie, a false witness breathes lies.
Matthew 22:39 You shall love your neighbor as yourself.	**Psalm 145:9** The LORD is good to all.	**Genesis 16:13** You are the God who sees.
Philippians 4:4 Rejoice in the Lord always. I will say it again: Rejoice!	**Numbers 6:24** The Lord bless you and keep you.	**Colossians 3:2** Set your minds on things above, not on earthly things.
Ephesians 4:30 And do not grieve the Holy Spirit.	**Colossians 3:16** Let the word of Christ dwell in you richly.	**1 John 5:3** This is love for God: to obey his commands.
Romans 10:13 Everyone who calls on the name of the Lord will be saved.	**Proverbs 3:5** Trust in the Lord with all your heart.	**Hebrews 13:8** Jesus Christ is the same yesterday, today and forever.
Psalm 150:6 Let everything that has breath praise the Lord.	**Romans 3:23** All people have sinned and come short of the glory of God.	**Matthew 5:14** You are the light of the world.

Psalm 145:9 The Lord is good to all.	**Colossians 3:20** Children, obey your parents in all things.	**James 1:17** Every good gift and every perfect gift is from above.
Matthew 28:20 I am with you always.	**1 John 3:23** Love one another.	**Psalm 56:3** "When I am afraid, I put my trust in You.
Ephesians 4:32 Be kind to one another.	**Psalm 119:105** Your word is a lamp to my feet and a light for my path.	**Psalm 118:24** This is the day the Lord has made; Let us rejoice and be glad in it.
Psalm 136:1 Give thanks to the Lord, for he is good. His love endures forever.	**Luke 6:31** Do to others as you would have them do to you.	**Philippians 4:13** "I can do all things through Christ who gives me strength."
Psalm 138:1 I will praise thee with my whole heart.	**John 10:11** I am the good shepherd.	**Matthew 6:24** No one can serve two masters.
Proverbs 30:5 Every word of God proves true.	**Ephesians 6:1** Children, obey your parents in the Lord, for this is right.	**John 11:35** Jesus wept.
Deuteronomy 6:5 You shall love the LORD your God with all your heart and with all your soul and with all your might.	**Corinthians 10:31** Whatever you do, do everything for the glory of God.	**Psalm 19:1** The heavens declare the glory of God.

Genesis 1:1 In the beginning, God created the heavens and the earth.	**Psalm 139:14** I praise you God, for I am fearfully and wonderfully made.	**Isaiah 43:5** Do not be afraid for I am with you.
Ecclesiastes 12:13 Fear God and keep his commandments.	**Matthew 28:6** He is not here, he is risen!	**Acts 5:29** We must obey God rather than men.
1 Thessalonians 5:17 Pray without ceasing.	**Isaiah 26:4** Trust in the Lord forever, for the Lord God is an everlasting rock.	**Psalm 46:10** Be still, and know that I am God.
Proverbs 2:6 The Lord gives wisdom.	**Psalm 1:6** The LORD knows the way of the righteous, but the way of the wicked will perish.	**Psalm 150:6** Let everything that has breath praise the LORD!
Galatians 6:7 Do not be deceived: God is not mocked, for whatever one sows, that will he also reap.		

Safety

Crossing a Street

Be careful when crossing the street. First, you must stop. Then, look to make sure no cars are coming. First, you look left, then right, then left again before crossing.

Protecting from Illness

Bathroom Etiquette

The proper etiquette for the bathroom is to be quiet, do your business, flush the toilet, and wash your hands. Make sure the paper towels are placed in the trash can. (Students should pratice how to wash their hands.) Incase there's no flush toilet, teach students that it is very important to wash their hands each time they use the tolet.

Don't Spread Germs

1. Cover your sneezes. If you don't sneeze into a tissue or your arm, you are spreading your germs everywhere.
2. Wash your hands. Turn on the water, get one pump of soap, and scrub. Then, rinse off all the soap bubbles, dry your hands with paper towels, turn off the water and throw the paper towel in the trash can.
3. Use hand sanitizer. Use one pump of hand sanitizer, that is plenty of sanitizer to clean your hands and not make a mess or waste it.

Protecting from Sexual Abuse

Hugs & Kisses

We don't ever give kisses at school. It is okay to give hugs at school, but you should always ask first. Make sure it is okay to hug someone instead of just hugging them.

Safe Touch

Safe touches are wanted and fun. They make us feel excited, loved, proud, and happy. Examples of safe touches are hug, high five, pat on the back, holding hands.

Bad Touch

Bad touches hurt us and are unwanted. They make us feel hurt, scare, sad, and angry.

Examples of **BAD** TOUCHES are hitting, punching, throwing things, pinching, kicking, and pushing.

Private Touch

Our private parts are covered by our underwear. Private touches are <u>unwanted</u>.

They happen when someone touches your private part or ask you to touch theirs. Private parts are called "private" because they are no one's business but our own.

They make us feel embarrassed, confused, disgusted and uncomfortable.

If someone tries to give me an Bad Touch or Private Touch, I am strong and brave. I look the person in the eye, I tell them, "No, Stop, I don't like that!" in a strong voice. Then I find a grown-up I trust and tell them what happened right away. BadTouches and Private Touches are never your fault. When you tell a safe person about someone hurting you or someone close to you, you are a hero!

<u>I am the boss of my body.</u>
<u>I decide who can touch me, where, and when.</u>

Motivating With Passion

What Makes a Teacher Great!

Proficient communication skills.
If a teacher's communication skills are good — verbal, nonverbal, and visual, which involve speaking, writing, imagery, body language, and the organization of ideas into understandable structures — they can convey knowledge with better skill and results.

Superior listening skills.
Good teachers also happen to be excellent listeners. "If speaking is silver, then listening is gold."

Knowledge and passion for teaching.
A teacher is only as good as what they know. Passion is infectious. The love of education inspires students to learn. The best teachers are those that clearly show the love and importance of education, and pass that passion and desire to learn on to their students.

Ability to build caring relationships with students.
A good teacher notices when even one student among many does not understand and makes an effort to communicate individually when necessary. A great teacher doesn't only teach from the head. In the best classrooms, hearts are involved, as well. Great teachers need to be able to build caring relationships with their students. It is the caring student-teacher relationship that facilitates the exchange of information.

Friendliness and approachability.
Because it's the teacher's job to help students learn, they must be easy to approach. Students will have questions that can't be answered if the teacher isn't friendly and easy to talk to. The crabby, unapproachable, terse, mean, arrogant, rude, all-business teacher don't make good impressions that last a lifetime. If the students think of their

teacher as their enemy, they certainly won't learn. The best teachers are the most open, welcoming, and easy to approach.

Outstanding preparation and organization skills.

Great teachers spend endless hours outside of the classroom preparing, designing lessons, learning more (both about their subject matter specifically and how to teach, in general), participating in professional development, and thinking of fresh and interesting ways to teach the students. Have excellent lesson plans, lectures, and assignments that they continually improve.

Good work ethic.

A great teacher will do almost anything to help their students. They always make time and are always willing to help. If something doesn't work, they'll work tirelessly until they find a solution. A teacher's work is never done, but the best ones never stop trying; they never quit.

Community-building skills.

The best teachers understand the importance of building supportive and collaborative environments. Great teachers foster healthy and mutually respectful relationships between the students. They know how to establish guidelines and assign roles to enlist every student's help and participation. Every student feels like they are not only accepted by the larger group, but that their presence is a necessary ingredient in the classroom's magic. Their classrooms are like little communities where each individual plays a part and feels at home.

High expectations for everyone.

A teacher's expectations have a huge impact on student achievement. The best teachers have high expectations for all of their students. They expect a lot from each student, but those expectations are both challenging and realistic. Great teachers strive to help each student attain their personal best.

How to be a Great Teacher

A teacher should serve as a role model for their students. Guide them and when the time is right, let them go as they need to face the world on their own. Being a teacher is like being a parent; you mold students from the start and push them a little bit further when they start to grow. Once they are old enough, give your best wishes and say goodbye. One day, when you two will meet again, you will be surprised by the flashbacks and memories you have undergone with each student and how you have affected his or her life.

1. Be a companion — Be a friend, but always know where you stand and where your limits are. You are a role-model; know when to switch. By this, we mean a teacher should know when is the proper time to be strict. Be their friend, but don't go too far. Help students with schoolwork, listen to them, talk about their lives, but remember you are their teacher.

2. Don't limit yourself to the chalkboard, make your lesson relevant to their lives — If the teacher is not only limited to the blackboard and actually tries to apply what or she is teaching to the students through an activity students can relate to, students might come to understand a certain topic better than before. If you want your students to remember your lessons, try to connect the information you provide with some moments of your students' lives.

3. Use as many different materials for your lessons as possible — Use books, videos, music, presentations, speeches, and everything that can be interesting for your students. Be patient, and explain your material over and over again, making sure all students understand what you're talking about. It would be difficult for them to learn further if they don't get the basics.

4. Be prepared to teach — Organizing time and preparing materials in advance are important in effective teaching. Know your content. Do the reading, take notes on the material, review lecture notes, prepare an outline to cover, make a list of ques-

tions to use, make a handout to discuss, design homework assignment or questions, compile bibliographies or other outside information related to the material, collect visual materials, prepare supplemental reading.

5. Manage the classroom effectively — Managing your classroom includes all the strategies a teacher uses to organize and arrange students, learning materials, space, and use of classroom time to maximize the efficiency of teaching and learning. Establishment fair, reasonable, enforceable, and consistently applied rules. To encourage a positive and orderly learning environment, establish a routine and system for daily tasks and requirements. Use classroom routines as a means of enforcing high standards for classroom behavior.

6. Believe in them — Students who do not believe in themselves tend to have more behavioral and academic problems. A good teacher instills confidence. Teachers who believe in their students and constantly push them to their limits, and appreciate what they are doing are the best ones. It is very important for a student to feel the support of his teacher and know, that he will always help when it is needed. Try to believe in everyone, and don't leave any of your students behind.

7. Don't stop learning — As a teacher, never close your doors to knowledge. Study more about your subject even if you are already a master of it. Don't limit yourself; adding additional knowledge to your lectures can amaze students and make them think that you are so smart, and slowly they can be influenced by you. Show them that you can still work and study at the same time.

Empowering Students

The act of empowering students is a process of guiding them to feel and believe that they are prevailing as youngsters. When we empower our young children with skills development, they are claiming their right to a decent living by being willing to take the role of leadership. Part of empowering our students is making sure they have the right to give their views and opinions about decisions that affect them and to be listened to. This develops a strong sense of self-esteem as they grow up. Teachers can play a major role in helping students find their voice; having the courage to speak up, express their opinions, (having opinions in the first place), help them discover what makes each of them unique, and help them to define their life goals.

How teachers can empower their students.

Practice positive reinforcement, and make it a positive experience. Positive reinforcement is anything that occurs after a behavior that increases the likelihood that the behavior will reoccur. You do not want to reward students for just doing what is expected. Be specific in your praise, especially when teaching something at the beginning. Consider what you want students to do and notice who is doing that well. Specify what it is that you like. Vary the recipients of your praise. Positive reinforcement improves behavior. Examples of positive reinforcement: giving high five, offering praise, giving a hug or pat on the back, giving a thumbs-up, clapping & cheering, and telling another adult how proud you are of the student's behavior while the student is listening.

Invite each student to lead: students should be asked to lead, whether they accept the offer or not. Don't force participation, inspire it. Spark participation with an engaging subject. Keep asking, throughout the year, and eventually, having watched others do it, the student will realize it's not really intimidating. Help students find their passion; passionate people don't remain quiet for long.

Allow creative expression: students should be given the freedom to voice what they think. Offer more engaging prompts by getting students to speak out on topics covered in class. Give more discussion time for students to explore and develop their ideas—

discussion enhances learning and memory. Support innovation, making something new will encourage them to continue thinking about new things. Encourage students to write down new ideas, at the moment, as they arise.

Recognize those students who speak out: pull students aside and let them know you appreciate their courage or refer to his/her comment later in a class discussion. It's the personal touch that is most rewarding. Encourage students to explain their views; if students can explain why they agree or disagree, they are one step closer to turning all those opinions into a single voice.

Make lessons personally relevant: it is easier for students to see where their voice might fit into a situation if that situation is relevant to their daily lives. Share inspiring stories, yours or someone else's. The more successful self-expression students see, the more likely they are to try it themselves.

Allow students to disagree with you: make sure they feel comfortable enough to express their opinion. Encourage casual debate, a debate is one of the best excuses to exercise your voice. Reward risk-takers, a student will find their voice much more quickly if they aren't afraid of taking risks. Welcome feedback on your teaching, one of the best ways to show your student's voice matter.

Be a better listener: no matter how good we are, we can always be better. Your student's voice depends on it. Inquire— think —reflect is a great voice-strengthening exercise. Have students ask questions on a topic, consider possible answers, and evaluate the accuracy of each answer.

From time to time, let each student solve a unique problem without making it a competition. This allows students to feel personally connected and responsible for their own issues.

Promote research as a class project: or an independent project. An opinion backed by research makes for a stronger voice. Brainstorm with your students. Be a part of the process in order to treat all voices equally. It is important to show your students that you do not have all the answers. Having a voice doesn't mean you are always right.

Recognize performance and progress. Make sure students know the difference between the two and help them understand what you expect. Students can be successful on tasks in class but learn virtually nothing; conversely, students can do relatively poorly on those same tasks but learn quite a lot. Performance is short-term, and progress is long-term. Teachers won't know if their students have actually learned something until after a period of time in which the students didn't use or think about the information. Teachers can evaluate how effective their instructions are by setting the goals, teach, then measure the student's progress toward meeting the goals each week.

Have patience and let each student finish their thoughts. Don't immediately step in when they are struggling with words. Help students determine what they want. Knowing what you want can lead to knowing what you think. Feeling motivated will help to express it. Build respect for the student's opinion. The student's voice doesn't have to be 'right' or 'popular', but it does have to reflect self-respect. Emphasize that no one gets to know how they feel or what they want if they don't express themself.

Explore different forms of leadership: leadership can come from art, or teaching others something they know. Teach a lesson on freedom of speech—finding your voice is supported by the law. Emphasize the right to voice their opinion, students should understand that they have a basic right to voice their opinions. Encourage emulation; the best and brightest learn form the best and brightest before them.

Provide a platform (whether your students like writing, speaking, or building), you'll need to support their means of self-expression with an appropriate platform.

Holidays in Liberia

January 1	New Year's Day
February 11	Armed Forces Day
Second Wednesday of March	Decoration Day
March 15	J. J. Roberts' Birthday
Second Friday of April	Fast and Prayer Day
May 14	National Unification Day
July 26	Independence Day
August 24	Flag Day
First Thurdsay of November	Thanksgiving Day
November 29	President William V.S. Tubman's Birthday
December 25	Christmas Day

Flag of Liberia

Seal of Liberia

Liberia (Monrovia)

Bomi — Tubmanburg
Bong — Gbarnga
Gbarpolu — Bopolu
Grand Bassa — Buchanan
Grand Cape Mount — Robertsport
Grand Gedeh — Zwedru
Grand Kru — Barclayville
Lofa — Voinjama
Margibi — Kakata
Maryland — Harper
Montserrado — Bensonville
Nimba — Sanniquellie
Rivercess — River Cess
River Gee — Fish Town
Sinoe — Greenville

Conversion Table

MILE TO KILOMETER
1 = 1.6 kilometer
5 miles = 8.0 kilometers
10 miles = 16.0 kilometers
20 miles = 32.1 kilometers

MASS AND WEIGHT
Metric and Customary
1 gram = 1,000 milligrams
1 kilogram = 1,000 grams
1 pound = 16 ounces
1 ton = 2,000 pounds

TIME
1 minute = 60 seconds
1 hour = 60 minutes
1 day = 24 hours
1 week = 7 days
1 year = 12 months
1 year = 52 weeks
1 year = 365 days

LENGTH
Metric and Customary
1 kilometer = 1,000 meters
1 meter = 100 centimeters
1 meter = 1,000 millimeters
1 centimeter = 10 millimeters
1 foot = 12 inches
1 yard = 3 feet
1 mile = 1,760 yards
1 mile = 5,280 feet

CAPACITY
Metric and Customary
1 liter = 1,000 milliliters
1 cup = 8 fluid ounces
1 pint = 2 cups
1 quart = 2 pints
1 gallon = 4 quarts

Academic Journal

Year: _____ - _____

Rural Community: _____

County: _____

Emergency Contact: _____

Phone Number: _____

Schedule

Class	Monday	Tuesday	Wednesday	Thursday	Friday

Lesson Plans & Events

August	September	October

November	December	January

February	March	April

May	June	July

Notes:

No Child Left Behind

Teacher Jeanette is an initiative that emphasized the academic development of young children by making available books and workbooks that help parents and teachers inspire literacy and learning for children in African developing countries. We publish academic books students can relate to culturally.

We help to meet the basic needs of primary education for children living in an orphanage and rural communities. It is our goal to provide updated education to children without access to quality education. Visit our website for more information — www.liberialiterarysociety.org

Kinder Kollege Curriculum Details
Our Kinder Kollege 2-year curriculum, is suggested for a Teacher-to-student ratio of 1 teacher to 25 students and includes nine Teacher Jeanette Kinder Kollege workbooks (math, science, social studies, Bible stories, language arts, reading, writing, spelling, technology, and handwriting), and a backpack with school supplies. For more information, visit our website at — www.teacherjeanette.com

Kinder Kollege Workbooks
Pre-K to Kindergarten

Teacher Jeanette Workbooks and Other Children's Books

These books are available everywhere books are sold. For information on wholesale purchase for individuals, private schools and organizations, please contact: villagetalespub@gmail.com

GETTING STARTED WITH ABC & 123

Primer Spelling List

Learning Objectives
Students should be able to spell most of these words at the end of the school year.

Ant	Hen	Sit
Ax	Hut	Six
Bat	Ice	Sun
Bed	Jar	Ten
Big	Key	Tree
Bird	Leg	Tub
Box	Lion	Van
Bug	Mat	Wig
Cow	Mud	Win
Cup	Nest	Xray
Dog	Net	Yam
Egg	Owl	Zebra
Fish	Pan	Zoo
Fix	Pen	
Fox	Pig	
Fun	Pin	
Goat	Queen	
Hat	Rat	

www.ingramcontent.com/pod-product-compliance
Lightning Source LLC
Chambersburg PA
CBHW080448170426
43196CB00016B/2722